HIGHER PURPOSE
VENTURE CAPITAL

FIFTY VENTURE-BACKED STARTUPS THAT ARE UPLIFTING HUMANITY
THROUGH SOCIAL AND FINANCIAL INCLUSION

RON LEVIN

SEACOAST
PRESS

Published by SEACOAST PRESS
1 New Hampshire Ave | Suite 125 | Portsmouth, NH 03801 | USA
603-546-2812 | https://www.seacoastpress.com/

Printed in the United States of America
ISBN-13: 978-1-960142-38-2

DEDICATION

In loving memory of the first author I ever met—
my mom, Betty Bergman Levin (Z"L).
Dedicated to my father, Amos Levin, and to Toma, Valentina, and Maya.

ENDORSEMENT

For investors seeking to invest in social impact ventures or who view investment with an inclusive and equitable lens, this is a must read. Ron not only gives readers a practical "how to" manual on how to become a savvy social impact investor, but I can personally attest to the fact that he follows his own advice and walks the talk. The companies he invests in are companies not only with a social impact focus but these are companies addressing some of society's most vexing problems. No investor who is interested in social impact investing should do so before reading Ron's book.

—Colette A.M. Phillips, President of Colette Phillips Communications, Founder of the social Impact Venture, Get Konnected!, and co-founder of the GK Fund, a social impact investment fund.

Knowing what we know about the inherent inequities and barriers to entry for diverse founders, Ron Levin's book is a testimony to creating pathways to inclusive entrepreneurship, showcasing bold founders and investors who are building scalable solutions to solve today's big problems.

—Maggie Sanchez, Project Director - Race, Gender, Equity & Entrepreneurship, Harvard Business School

This visionary page turner shares inspiring examples of companies actively closing the gap between the "haves" and "have nots." With a bifocal lens on profitability and social good, Levin introduces the reader to businesses addressing both. His real-world perspective as an accomplished entrepreneur and investor makes this is a must read for those tired of hearing excuses and seeking practical models that grow the economic pie for all.

—Selena Cuffe, Chief Growth Officer, Blackstone Consulting, Inc., and Co-Founder, Heritage Link Brands, LLC

Ron Levin has made crystal clear with these concise and compelling cases that it is possible—as he argues, even imperative—for VCs to do well by doing good. Ron also intriguingly throws down the gauntlet to his unregulated and elitist VC peers (my words, not his) to ignore these investments at their—and our common—peril.

—Daniel Isenberg, PhD, former professor, Harvard Business School, and author, *Worthless, Impossible and Stupid*

By profiling inspiring, mission-driven companies and their founders, Ron Levin is showing us—not telling us—about business's critical role in driving social change. These real-life examples serve as a call to action and help us chart the path to a more equitable and sustainable market.

—Alexandra Baillie, President, Good & Well

CONTENTS

INTRODUCTION

THE WEALTH GAP

> "Poverty is not just a lack of money; it is not having the
> capability to realize one's full potential as a human being."
> —Abhijit V. Banerjee and Esther Duflo (co-recipients of 2019
> Nobel Memorial Prize in Economic Sciences), *Poor Economics:*
> *A Radical Rethinking of the Way to Fight Global Poverty*

I t's astonishing that in a wealthy nation such as the United States, which in 2022 produced a gross domestic product per capita of $76,648, we should be talking about poverty. But we are. According to the U.S. Census, in that same year, 12.8 percent of our citizens, comprising roughly 43 million men, women, and children, lived in poverty.

What is poverty? The government uses a formula to calculate income, and in 2021 the threshold was $27,750 for a family of four. Try supporting a family on that amount! Unless you're literally living off the land, it cannot be done.

In the United States, the problem is not the *amount* of wealth generated by our citizens, which in 2022 reached an astonishing $26 trillion. That amounts to roughly $70,000 per citizen on average, but the distribution of that wealth is far from equitable. Household income inequality is growing. While there are many ways to measure it, the bottom line is this, as summarized by the Pew Research Center:

"The growth in income in recent decades has tilted to upper-income households. At the same time, the U.S. middle class, which once comprised the clear majority of Americans, is shrinking. Thus, a greater share of the nation's aggregate income is now going to upper-income households and the share going to middle- and lower-income households is falling."[1]

The "poverty penalty" describes the phenomenon that poor people tend to pay more to eat, buy, and borrow than the rich. The term became widely known through a 2005 book by C.K. Prahalad, *The Fortune at the Bottom of the Pyramid,* and helps explain why it is so common in societies for the rich to get richer while the poor get poorer. For example, a poor person will pay a much higher interest rate to borrow $1,000 from a lender than a rich person will pay to borrow $1 million from that same lender. It's a vicious cycle to break out of when one's cards dealt in life include no access to financial credit, no access to or ability to afford high-quality schools and educational opportunities, and no access to the best healthcare available. There is food insecurity, a lack of affordable housing and childcare, limited transportation options to pursue more lucrative opportunities, and a societal culture where the "haves" always have a leg up.

The problem is global. Oxfam reports that since 1995, the top 1 percent of the world's population possess almost 20 times more of global wealth compared to the bottom 50 percent of humanity.

Meanwhile, to add insult to injury, the world's wealthiest one percent produce double the carbon emissions of the bottom 50 percent.

The results of such gaping holes of inequality are incalculable. You've heard of Maslow's Hierarchy of Needs. It's a pyramid with five ascending levels of human needs: physiological (food and clothing), safety (job security), love and belonging needs (friendship), esteem, and self-actualization. People generally cannot ascend from a lower need, such as physiological, unless that need has been fulfilled. For example, you cannot hope to reach a level of esteem in your community if you're struggling to meet your basic needs of food and shelter.

The very base of Maslow's Hierarchy relates to the cost of shelter and nourishment and the cycle of poverty. When children don't have adequate schools, they do not advance into more skilled, rewarding professions later in life. If parents don't have access to preschool and infant childcare without giving up their job, they cannot adequately provide for their families. It is about crime, imprisonment, and recidivism. It is about basic health, wellness, and personal care. It is about being able to access capital or goods in a time of need or to pursue new opportunities, such as starting a small business.

According to Oxfam, at least 21,300 people each day die globally as a consequence of inequality. The causes are hunger, lack of access to healthcare (including mental health), gender-based violence, as well as effects of climate change, such as rising sea levels and natural disasters. According to the Bureau of Labor Statistics, in the United States, weekly earnings on average for a college graduate are more than double that of a high school dropout. Nearly all who do not complete high school drop out for reasons that, in one way or another, tie back to wealth inequality. The ripple effects of living in a continuous poverty cycle are immense and impact society at large. As merely one example cited by Michelle Alexander in *The New Jim Crow*, in the U.S., two-thirds detained in jails reported annual income of under $12,000 prior to incarceration.[2]

There are many people who would argue that capitalism itself is the cause of wealth inequality; and it's undeniable that some wealth inequality is a built-in feature of the system. To be honest, it's a *benefit* of the system, because inequality serves as a driver of innovation and achievement. Every society needs people who say to themselves, "I can work harder and acquire more wealth, and my work will contribute to the growth of the economy."

But too much of a gap between the minority rich and the majority poor—which we see in many developing nations—provides fertile ground for corruption and crime. It's not good for anyone. In the United States from about 1937 to 1947, a period dubbed as the "Great Compression," the income gap between the rich and poor closed dramatically. With a strong middle class, it stayed relatively small until the 1980s, when it began to widen—and it's only gotten worse. In 2018, the United Nations reported that the U.S. had the highest income inequality in the Western world, with vast numbers of middle-class Americans "perched on the edge," and with 40 percent of adults saying they could not cover an unexpected $400 expense. "The share of the top 1 percent of the population in the United States has grown steadily in recent years," the report notes. "In relation to both wealth and income the share of the bottom 90 percent has fallen in most of the past 25 years."[3]

The gap has been caused by many things, including government policies. But to those who would say that capitalism itself is to blame, impact investors can reply, "Capitalism can be the *solution*." Rather than imposing the heavy hand of government, individual and group investors can exert tremendous leverage to direct their dollars into companies that share their humanistic values.

Let's see how this can be done.

CAPITAL AND CORPORATIONS

In our capitalist society, corporations owned by citizen shareholders provide the goods and services we need every day. Traditionally, these corporations and their investors have been motivated by a mix of altruism and profit motive. For example, while a bread maker may take pride in his product and take satisfaction knowing it feeds people, to stay in business he needs to earn a profit from his investment. His cash profit must be distributed among the investors who have put up the money to launch the business. If he fails to provide this, his shareholders will demand to be repaid with assets from the company itself—meaning, foreclosure.

Capitalism works best when these two impulses—altruism and profit—are balanced. Throughout history, the greatest and most successful capitalists have introduced and sold innovative products and services that have transformed people's lives. Probably the first truly transformative capitalist was Henry Ford, who, at the dawn of the 20th century, produced and sold the Model T automobile. Notwithstanding his contemptible bigotry of the highest order, Ford's sincerely held vision was to provide cheap and relatively clean transportation for anyone, and in pursuit of his mission, over the product life cycle of the Model T, he *reduced* the price from $825 in 1909 to a low of $265 in 1924—about $4,600 today. He also raised wages in 1913 from $2.34 per day to $5 per day for his assembly line workers, which allowed them to actually buy the vehicles they made.

But how about the other side of the equation—the profits? Did the Ford Motor Company turn a profit for its investors? Of course it did, and the company remains a $150 billion-plus revenue machine a full century later.

THE COMMUNITY AS SILENT INVESTOR

Over the past century, we've seen the balance between altruism and profit swing back and forth. In the 1960s, just as American corporations, which had dominated the globe after the Second World War, were facing new competition from foreign competitors, particularly an emergent Japan, industrial theorists began to promote the idea that a company that pursued *any* socially responsible policies was a traitor to the cause of capitalism. These theorists argued that a company's sole and exclusive obligation was to return every possible dollar of profit to its cash investors. For a manager to spend company money on anything not directly related to generating profits from sales was a misuse of funds. The idea was that the shareholders should be first in line at the profit-sharing table, and that any manager who failed to do this was not fulfilling his or her fiscal obligations.

This position represented a swing of the pendulum too far in the direction of taking profits for the company at the expense of the community. This is because, in a sense, the community in which a company is located is a *silent investor in that company*. All companies, large and small, are consumers of community resources—air, water, soil, energy, highways, bridges, railroads, subways, police, fire, and the Internet. In addition, it's an axiom that capitalism can only thrive in a society where there is the rule of law and a system of civil justice. These assets cost money, and companies need to factor this reality into their bottom line.

For example, a company that pollutes the air is a costly burden on the community in which it exists. Why should its shareholders enjoy the excess profits which are being subsidized by taxpayers? It would be fair to have a mechanism by which the cost of cleaning the polluted air is put into the budget of the company. Or how about the global retailer—you know who they are—which pays its workers less than a living wage, forcing them to accept government assistance, which in turn comes out of the pockets of taxpayers. The local taxpayers are silent investors because they help subsidize the company's operations.

Responsible advocates of capitalism see the value in altruism and understand that businesses cannot be just blind profit machines but should take their rightful place as stewards of their community, with obligations to *all* their stakeholders, not just the shareholders. Acting in a socially responsible manner is not an act of charity; it's a fiduciary duty.

The argument that companies must consider only the enrichment of the shareholders, while ignoring the substantial contribution by the community as silent investor, is easily dismantled.

1. **A shareholder may have invested more than cash into the enterprise—and may want the company to be socially responsible.** In many companies, holders of large blocks of stock are often the founders, who may have contributed little money but significant amounts of sweat equity and the critical ideas that launched the enterprise. Jeff Bezos, the founder of Amazon, is a perfect example. As of this writing, he owns 9.73 percent of the company's stock, yet he put relatively little of his own cash into the venture. Yes, such people are "managers," but they are also owners, and they are entitled to voice their opinion as to how the company's assets should be managed.

2. **Many shareholders are concerned with more than the fastest possible cash return.** Today's world is full of thoughtful, smart people who look at the bigger picture. They're concerned about receiving a good return on their investment (who wouldn't be?), but they actually care about how that return was earned. They recognize the irrefutable fact that the community is a silent investor deserving of representation.

3. **Socially responsible businesses can be just as profitable as regressive businesses.** Perhaps the biggest mistake is the assertion that managers who invest in socially responsible aspects of the enterprise are less astute or less mindful of profitability than those who are concerned only with the immediate, end-of-quarter cash return. This is ridiculous. In fact, as we'll see in the pages ahead, the companies that provide substantial returns *year after year* are often those that make investments in their people, their environment, and their community.

Even with the necessity of the profit motive—which is non-negotiable—there's an absolute bottom line, in the form of two questions posed to an investor:

"Do you want to use your investment funds to help make the world a better place while fairly sharing in the rewards of doing so?

"If you were ninety years old and your grandchild came to you and asked, 'What did you do with your money?' what would you say?"

B CORPS AND BENEFIT CORPORATIONS

We have seen in recent years the emergence of the B Corp certification and the closely related benefit corporation company structure. B Corporation (also B Lab or B Corp) is a private certification of for-profit companies based on their social and environmental performance. The certification is awarded by B Lab, a global nonprofit organization with offices in the United States, Europe, Canada, Australia and New Zealand, and a partnership in Latin America with Sistema B.

Founded in 2006 in Berwyn, Pennsylvania, B Lab is a nonprofit organization that created and awards the B Corporation certification. It is not a government agency. The "B" stands for "beneficial" and indicates that the certified organizations voluntarily meet certain standards of transparency, accountability, sustainability, and performance, with the goal to create value for society, not just for traditional stakeholders such as the shareholders.

Companies must re-certify every three years to retain B Corporation status. As of September 2022, there are 5,697 certified B Corporations across 158 industries in eighty-five countries.

In contrast a *benefit corporation* or B corporation in the United States (or in several jurisdictions, a public-benefit corporation [PBC]) is a for-profit corporate entity authorized by 35 U.S. states and the District of Columbia. A B corporation's legally defined goals include a positive impact on society, its employees, the community, and the environment, in addition to returning a profit. In contrast to a traditional C corporation, activist shareholders cannot attack the board of a benefit corporation if it engages in socially responsible practices because such practices are built into the mission of the company.

This brings us to the immediate topic of this book: venture capital and its role in our modern society.

Venture capital fundamentally exists as a means of channeling capital to enable promising entrepreneurs to deliver on their goals of creating scalable and innovative solutions to existing problems and gaps in a market, while at the same time delivering outsized returns on investment. Some of these problems that technology-focused founders address are of a profound societal nature, and while those problems seemingly may not always correlate with the highest potential for investor return, a generation of emerging entrepreneurs are showing the fallacy in that thinking.

Higher Purpose Venture Capital is intended to seek out and learn from founders of venture-backed mission-driven startup companies that are helping to solve the problems created by wealth inequality and societal injustice existing among those who are at an economic disadvantage. These problems will not be solved top-down but rather with creative ideas that come from the source of these challenges. As Professor Prahalad argued, "The problem of poverty must force us to innovate, not claim rights to impose our solutions."

ESG INVESTING MAKES A DIFFERENCE

Impact-oriented venture capital investing is not new. There are professionally managed venture capital funds, loosely organized angel groups, private investors, and family offices that focus on many types of venture investing with a "double bottom line" purpose. Many are becoming committed to environmental, social, and governance (ESG) investing, which refers to socially conscious investors using a set of standards for a company's behavior to screen potential investments.

As Investopedia defines it, "Environmental criteria consider how a company safeguards the environment, including corporate policies addressing climate change. Social criteria examine how it manages relationships with employees, suppliers, customers, and the communities where it operates."

Governance deals with a company's leadership, executive compensation, audits, internal controls, and shareholder rights.

ESG investment kicked off in the 1960s. While the ethical concerns may have changed since then, the heart of sustainable investing remains unchanged, and more and more investors are adopting ESG as a way to evaluate investment opportunities alongside more traditional analysis options.

While the term ESG is often used in the context of investing, the wider stakeholder universe of customers, suppliers, and employees are increasingly interested in the sustainability of an organization's operations.

In our economy, we're seeing a massive wealth transfer from the Baby Boomer generation to their children and grandchildren. According to a recent report by CNBC, this transfer will be as much as $68 trillion, and the people inheriting that wealth seem keenly interested in how that money should be invested.[4]

The ESG investing market is growing. As reported by PwC, asset managers globally are expected to increase their ESG-related assets under management (AUM) to $33.9 trillion by 2026, up dramatically from $18.4 trillion in 2021. With a projected compound annual growth rate (CAGR) of 12.9 percent, ESG assets are expected to reach 21.5 percent of total global AUM by 2027. According to PwC's *Asset and Wealth Management Revolution 2022* report, we're seeing a dramatic and continuing shift in the asset and wealth management (AWM) industry. In fact, nine of ten asset managers surveyed by PwC stated that integrating ESG into their investment strategy would improve overall returns. At the same time, fully 60 percent reported that ESG investing had already resulted in higher performance yields compared to non-ESG equivalents. Three-quarters of investors now consider ESG to be part of their fiduciary duties.[5]

The orientation toward impact-focused investing among large fund managers and their limited partners is highlighted in Apax Partners founder Sir Ronald Cohen's 2020 book, *Impact: Reshaping Capitalism to Drive Real Change*. He cites, as one example, the Government Pension Investment Fund (GPIF) of Japan, which manages the largest pool of retirement savings in the world. From January 2015 until March 2020, the chief investment officer was Hiromichi Mizuno, who dramatically shaped the fund's philosophy toward ESG investing. In 2019, he told *Bloomberg*, "Failing to integrate ESG factors is against the fiduciary duty, especially for clients who have long-term horizons... The other question is whether making extra returns is the only way to satisfy one's fiduciary duty. Our view of integrating ESG is not about beating the market but about making the capital markets more sustainable. ESG can be a catalyst to promote the sustainability of markets."[6]

UBS Group AG is a Swiss-based multinational bank and financial services company with assets under management exceeding $1 trillion. In October 2019, UBS joined the UN's Global Investors for Sustainable Development Alliance (GISD) and committed to raise $5 billion of SDG-related impact investments by the end of 2021. As the world's leading private bank, it aims to create a measurable positive social and environmental impact.

Today, stated goals of UBS include delivering investment products that support impact and socially, responsible themes; supporting the transition to a low-carbon economy in advisory and capital markets including supporting issuance of green and sustainable bonds; working towards full integration of ESG into investment research, and making sustainability the everyday standard across the firm.

In 2021, the Dow Jones Sustainability Index recognized UBS as the industry leader for the sixth year running.[7]

Founded in 1992 in San Francisco, California, and based in Fort Worth, Texas, TPG Inc. (formerly known as Texas Pacific Group) is an American private equity, buyout and growth equity firm. With $120 billion in AUM, the firm invests in a range of industries, including consumer/retail, media and telecommunications, industrials, technology, travel, leisure, and health care, and manages investment funds in growth capital, venture capital, public equity, and debt investments.

TPG first adopted a Global ESG Performance Policy in 2012 and became a signatory to the UN Principles of Responsible Investment in 2013. Each year, the company continues to strengthen and deepen the integration of ESG performance throughout the firm. As the company says, "At TPG, our priority for fostering strong environmental, social, and governance performance in our portfolio and in our operations is a long-standing core tenet of who we are as a firm. We have long held that it is simply good business."[8]

Family offices are significant players in the investment industry. There are thousands of them across the United States, Europe, and Asia. The biggest is Walton Enterprises, LLC, which in 2022 had over $224 billion in assets. The interesting thing about family offices is that they answer to no one except their owners, who can direct them any way they please. Younger family members are increasingly interested in making responsible investing an integral part of the family's mission and legacy, and they're leaning into ESG.

"Aligning investment practices with ESG goals allows high net worth families to establish a purposeful legacy that extends beyond lasting wealth," remarked Anthony DeCandido, an ESG advisory services partner at RSM US LLP, an audit, tax, and consulting firm and a member of the global accounting network RSM International. "There is also strong empirical research showing ESG can increase investment performance, so family offices should view ESG program adoption as smart business."[9]

In the past several years since I became a full-time venture capital investor with Alumni Ventures, I have been actively co-investing in at least twenty-five early-stage companies per year that run the gamut from seed to growth stage as well as covering sectors ranging from traditional SaaS to e-commerce, consumer, mobility, life sciences, quantum computing, and more.

Our job as venture capitalists is to identify highly promising companies that address problems or inefficiencies in large markets and that have management teams with the skills and temperament to scale these ideas into profitable global enterprises. A significant subset of these companies is particularly meaningful to me because the problems they are solving are so big and the solutions are both innovative and demonstrating truly impactful results that are helping real people in the real world.

A common theme across many of the more impactful deals I've worked on has been the creative solutions that address problems faced by those with limited economic means and opportunity for upward mobility.

TOWARD A BRIGHT FUTURE

While problems of income inequality and poverty are stark, the solutions to many of them are real and viable to scale, both in the U.S. and globally. This book profiles early-stage technology-driven companies that are making inroads on solutions to the problems of wealth inequality and serving the shocking level of humanity who struggle to keep up at the bottom of the pyramid.

In *The Fortune at the Bottom of the Pyramid*, Professor C.K. Prahalad revealed the innumerable societal ills brought on by those with money and power who do not understand or address the needs of the "have-nots." In demonstrating that businesses can profit by serving the lowest income earners,

Prahalad provided evidence for not overlooking opportunities where businesses have often neglected them. Beyond just serving these markets, however, creative entrepreneurs of today are increasingly focusing on empowering lower-income earners and those surviving at poverty levels to overcome barriers that have existed for generations.

For those who harbor the erroneous belief that investing in businesses serving low-income markets cannot be profitable, we can point to several venture capital funds that have done exactly that and have produced impressive returns. For example, Bridges Fund Management was founded in 2002 by Philip Newborough, Michelle Gliddens, and Sir Ronald Cohen to become a growth capital vehicle targeting market-rate returns by investing in businesses with a positive social or environmental impact and located in the poorest 25 percent of the United Kingdom. The company launched the Bridges U.S. Sustainable Growth Fund in 2015 to invest in lower middle-market U.S. growth companies solving environmental and social challenges.

Bridges Fund Management has posted strong results: In 2019, Bridges' total funds raised in the U.S. and U.K. surpassed the $1 billion mark. Through 2017, the fund delivered an average net annual return of 17 percent. Today, the fund boasts fourteen impact-driven funds and 160 portfolio investments.[10]

This book will reveal early-stage venture capital-backed companies operating in the realms of both early and adult education, as well as health and wellness, financial independence, affordable housing, food security, transportation, empowerment for the disabled, philanthropy enablement, and other areas. Some of the entrepreneurs that are featured are drawn from companies that I have invested in either personally or as part of Alumni Ventures.

For example, there is SoLo Funds, which is disrupting the notorious payday lending industry by democratizing access to emergency capital.

There is Aprende Institute, making practical skills training more accessible and affordable for Spanish speakers in both the U.S. and Latin America.

We will examine AllHere, which built a communication platform that leverages artificial intelligence to combat student absenteeism in public schools.

We'll also look at Vincere Health, a Harvard-incubated company that provides through its app and handheld device a suite of coaching, monitoring and financial incentives to encourage people to quit smoking and lead healthier lifestyles. All these businesses are proving to be both effective at their missions and highly scalable.

While the issue of wealth inequality is acute close to home in the U.S. and where many of these companies originate, we will not be limited to national borders. Many of the income inequality problems that we face stateside play out at a far grander scale overseas, particularly in developing countries. Some of the problems these startups address will correlate with race and gender inequality, while others may have different societal root causes, such as treatment of urban versus rural populations or entrenched caste systems, both explicit and implicit.

This book is fundamentally a learning journey borne out of my own curiosity and desire to be impactful in my work as an investor, advisor, and entrepreneur. Those who wish to ride along and contribute to our learning are warmly welcome to participate in this conversation about how venture capital can help empower entrepreneurs who aim to serve a higher purpose.

1

DEMOCRATIZING ACCESS TO MONEY AND CREDIT

A bank is a financial institution that is licensed to accept deposits from the public and creates a demand deposit while simultaneously making loans. Individual states, as well as the national government, regulate these banks. In recent decades, banks have broadened their product lines to become like supermarkets for financial services. From many banks you can "buy" anything from a retirement plan to a mortgage to insurance.

If you're wealthy and have low debt, banks work very well. They can make enough profit from lending out your money to borrowers to be happy with your patronage. But if you're a low-income person with only a few bucks in your bank account, that's not enough for the bank to make a robust profit. So the bank will find other ways to make money from you. They do this by charging fees. For example, they'll process your check payments in a certain order to maximize the number of overdrafts and therefore the multiple overdraft fees they could charge. They'll delay recognition of an incoming payment that you knew would cover a check you wrote, so that your check will bounce and incur a fee. There are fees for using an ATM, monthly maintenance fees, wire transfer fees, early account closing fees.

And if you have no credit history or account with an established bank, then you cannot get a loan. You won't qualify for a big loan, and small loans— or microloans—of just a few hundred dollars are simply not profitable. Too often, people who need a low-dollar loan to get their car fixed or pay the electric bill have no choice but to resort to a payday loan, which are often usurious and put the borrower deeper in debt.

The digital era has upended this traditional business model. How? A digital financial technology (fintech) company can operate with far lower costs than a traditional bank and earn a profit on small accounts and loans. These disruptors, often referred to as "neobanks," can build their IT platforms from scratch and develop new digital services that are difficult for incumbents with decades-old legacy platforms. Fintech companies can offer services that undercut those offered by traditional banks, such as low-dollar loans with fast approval, speedy new account creation with no branch visit required, the instant issuance and activation of cards through digital wallets like Apple Pay, free or low-fee money transfer, smartphone apps—all without having to gouge the customer with exorbitant fees.

The global outlook for investing in fintech is very positive. Multiple subsectors are poised to evolve while new ones emerge and flourish, and of course, the big banks aren't sitting still. They're increasing their digital services, leveraging artificial intelligence (AI) to improve the customer experience, and integrating cloud services to improve legacy system capabilities, better manage the vast amount of consumer data they handle, and increase the speed of data processing. The development of electronic wallets along with Google, Apple, and Samsung payment systems facilitated the move from cash and credit card payments to one click and contactless payment.

Here are some of the leading financial services companies working to democratize access to money and credit.

SOLO FUNDS

SoLo Funds provides a digital financial platform intended to efficiently conduct community marketplace lending for individual lenders and borrowers. The company's platform, which is available on both iOS and Android, leverages technology to assess the creditworthiness of individuals, enabling users to solve emergency cash needs with low-dollar-amount microloans on self-selected terms.

Headquarters and year founded: Los Angeles, 2017

Founder: Travis Holoway, co-founder and CEO, founded SoLo Funds alongside his friend and company chairman, Rodney Williams. Prior to founding SoLo, Travis built his career in the financial services industry with Northwestern Mutual. It was then that he discovered a major disconnect between the wealthy clients he met with daily and the vast number of Americans who live paycheck to paycheck. He felt that there were many pain points being experienced by individuals in the middle and lower ends of the financial spectrum that were being ignored and desperately needed to be addressed. Travis is a graduate of the University of Cincinnati and has been quoted in various publications and websites, including Forbes, American Banker, Black Enterprise, PYMNTS, and the LA Business Journal.

Funds raised and VC investors: $14.5 million from ACME Capital, Alumni Ventures, CEAS, Endeavor Catalyst, Impact America Fund, MaC Venture Capital, Serena Ventures, Techstars, West Ventures.

Q&A WITH THE FOUNDER

Where did the idea for SoLo originate?

My co-founder Rodney and I met in Cincinnati while I was in college and he was starting out at P&G. In subsequent years, while I was a wealth advisor at Northwestern Mutual and Rodney was founder of his other company LISNR, we both had similar experiences that led to a realization. Friends and family of ours recognized our early career success and came to us asking for small dollar loans of typically $50 to $250 to cover gas, utilities, emergency car repairs, and the like. We talked about these experiences and about the decision of whether to send money when friends or family are asking. People shouldn't have to do this as it puts stress and strain on relationships. You are damned if you do and damned if you don't in terms of what this can lead to between friends.

There is a lack of alternatives for short-term, small dollar loans. Payday loans, for example, are banned entirely in New York, leaving no good options for the borrower in need. If you don't get it from friends or family, you are simply left to go without. Even if someone does have access to payday loans, they are predatory in nature, with 400 percent annualized interest rates or higher being the norm.

On the flip side of this equation, we recognized that there are plenty of people with discretionary capital who are actively looking for yield. Many of those are also looking to have a positive social impact with their investments. We saw a solution in unlocking capital by pairing those who have it with those who have small cash needs. A great return potential is available to the lender side of the market. The whole goal is to have an equitable solution that empowers borrowers to have more control and autonomy. We want the best of both worlds.

What's the key problem that SoLo Funds intends to solve?

On the SoLo marketplace, borrowers create their own loan terms. They indicate how much they need and when they will pay it back. A borrower posts the request to our mobile marketplace, where another individual with discretionary capital can deploy capital directly to them. The lender can look at the borrower's history and find comfort in knowing that they are reliable. If a borrower hasn't paid a loan back, they are ineligible to borrow again. A lender can also look at a borrower's SoLo score and understand their ability to repay based on cash flow, how often they are paid, spending habits, etc.

How are you most differentiated as a service?

One important element of how the platform works is everything is transacted on debit rails instead of automated clearing house (ACH). This means funds can flow in real time. A borrower doesn't have to wait 2–3 business days but instead receives the money within seconds. The average loan on SoLo is funded in just 28 minutes. This is ideal for a borrower who is in a cash bind and needs money quickly. This is special and a big reason why we have been able to grow. The borrower sets their own loan terms within the marketplace and a stranger funds it. People hear about this through word-of-mouth as 65 percent of app store downloads come from direct search. Every user we get results in the acquisition of 5–6 new users. It has a strong organic halo, a key component of strong product-market fit.

What are the company's key accomplishments to date?

The SoLo platform has funded over 235,000 loans. In January 2022, we did 20,000 loans. We are accelerating very rapidly. By contrast, Lending Club funds just 7,000 per year, obviously at a very different average dollar amount, but a marketplace like this has never scaled so rapidly. Interestingly, 82 percent of transactions happen between lenders and borrowers who live in the very same zip code! People tend to live in areas where they are close to people of different economic means. Our users like that capital is being deployed and returns are recycled into the same communities. This is quite different from payday and title loans and even the traditional banking industry. The community banking premise used to be based on last name, status, and connections that get access to capital. We have lost that, and SoLo Funds is about redefining what community banking truly is. One last point is that we are the only Black-led certified B Corp in fintech in the U.S. or Canada. We firmly believe that we are the most equitable solution in space.

What lies ahead for SoLo?

For 2022, we are launching neobank services largely to make lending and borrowing on the platform more efficient. We will leverage a wallet that eases some of the strain the lenders face to issue capital. We are also looking at issuing debit cards, for example, to give faster access to capital. We intend to make our marketplace more efficient—as a wedge to neobanking services. Automated lending is also rolling out later this year.

Our goal is to build a community that enables financial autonomy for all. We're creating a path to upward financial mobility for our members, who can be both lenders and borrowers. We don't want people to be borrowers forever. In fact, 30 percent of our borrowers eventually become lenders on the platform. Our borrowers do not want to stay in their financial position forever. They look forward to paying it forward. We look forward to providing more financial services, such as credit cards, emergency savings funds, high interest savings accounts, insurance, and more.

We also have lenders who deploy capital but do not have a financial plan. Like Robinhood or Coinbase, we have people who come to SoLo seeking opportunities to earn yield, but many of them are skipping the basics. They are not investing in a 401K or an index fund but are going from ground zero straight into highly speculative, trendy investments like NFTs and purchasing "land" in the metaverse. They are skipping the basics and our goal is to provide more access to traditional tools for those who come to us to generate income, as well as those who come to satisfy short-term financial needs.

RON'S TAKE

The problem of having access to capital when it's urgently required has been confounding those in need since time immemorial. Those of means have historically had access to reputable banks and moneylenders. Those without have had to rely on less reliable and regulated sectors such as payday and title lenders that offer usurious interest rates on the order of several hundred percent annually, if not greater. Hence, the vicious cycle of wealth inequality. Those with little in the way of capital or collateral cannot achieve creditworthiness to obtain reasonable loans and must rely on tools that drive them further into a debt vortex. In more extreme scenarios, it can lead some who become desperate down even more troublesome paths.

SoLo is on the front lines of solving this issue from having identified that an efficient marketplace of borrowers and lenders is the best way to ensure fair and reasonable interest rates for both sides. No longer are schisms with families and friends needed for those uncomfortable moments in life when cash is short, and the need is imperative. The fact that 30 percent of SoLo's borrowers eventually become lenders is proof that more just economic tools are critical for uplifting and motivating advancement in wealth and financial independence. SoLo's impressive growth demonstrates that a free market, offered with transparency, fairness, and durability, can help to break the chains of economic injustice.

Disclaimer: Alumni Ventures invested in multiple financing rounds of SoLo Funds in 2021 and 2022.

ZIRTUE

Zirtue provides a lending application designed to enable users to digitize and mobilize loans between friends and family. The platform allows borrowers to request and automatically repay loans to any contact on the user's mobile. The borrower has the capability to set the loan amount while the lender establishes the repayment. The company's application features real-time integration with creditors to ensure direct payment and reliable repayment of funds.

Headquarters and year founded: Dallas, 2018

Founder: Dennis Cail II, co-founder and CEO, has deep experience expertise building, scaling, and investing in fintech platforms with exciting business models and teams of highly effective members. Prior to founding Zirtue, Dennis worked in leading organizations such as PwC and IBM Global Services. A retired Navy systems engineer with top secret clearance, Dennis received his bachelor's in computer science and an MBA from Southern Methodist University (SMU).

Funds raised and VC investors: $6.5 million from Capital Factory, Google for Startups, Mastercard, Mercury Fund, Morgan Stanley, Multicultural Innovation Lab, Northwestern Mutual Future Ventures, Reinventure Capital Fund, Revolution, SixThirty Ventures, Techstars.

Q&A WITH THE FOUNDER

Where did the idea for Zirtue originate?

I grew up in low-income public housing in Monroe, Louisiana, where there were no banks or credit unions. If people needed cash quickly, they would have their checks cashed at the liquor store and would have to pay a 30 percent fee. Even back then as a kid, I knew that didn't seem right. Later, when I left the Navy, I witnessed predatory lenders, charging interest of as much as 400 percent, targeting minorities, people with low income, and military veterans. I decided I wanted to start chipping away at this and create more fair and equitable access to capital.

What's the key problem that Zirtue intends to solve?

The primary alternative to payday lending for urgent cash needs that I have witnessed directly within my community is that friends and family seek to borrow money from one another. Unfortunately, this can create a lot of awkwardness and often limited success of the lender in getting repaid the loans as they had agreed with the borrower. It is then the lender who often comes out as the "bad guy" when attempting to recover their loan. Zirtue was created to bake transparency and accountability into the process. Our business model is driven by the mission to build financial inclusion one relationship at a time by formalizing and simplifying loans one family at a time.

How are you most differentiated as a service?

The Zirtue application creates a digital paper trail of loans, including a promissory note. We link a user's bank and debit card to their profile. Users can schedule automatic monthly drafts and we take responsibility for sending nudges or adding new payment methods when needed. We are also differentiated in that we give borrowers the option to pay specific creditors directly whom we partner with, such as AT&T and healthcare providers. The lender can also see if their funds are being used for their intended purposes through our bill pay transparency. We essentially give our lenders more ways to say yes to friends and family.

We like to think of ourselves as being in a relationship business where our users do not have to pay 400 percent interest rates and our lenders can feel good about providing capital in a more responsible way, while not being taken advantage of. In addition, our enterprise creditor customers are better able to capture at-risk dollars and create a better customer experience. The last thing they want to do is send a customer into collections or discontinue their services.

What are the company's key accomplishments to date?

Over 300,000 people have used our platform. Zirtue processed over $30 million in loans last year, which was three times more than the year before. We believe we can get to $200 million in loans this year, all without spending money on marketing. We provide our application entirely for free to both lenders and borrowers and we make money through the collections that we offer to our large enterprise customers.

What lies ahead for Zirtue?

Americans lend and borrow over $200 billion per year, a rate that is growing 30 percent annually. We intend to continue building services that help friends and family to make transactions in a simpler way. Later this year, as one example of a new feature, we plan to introduce the option for users to report to credit bureaus to help them establish or repair credit. We will also be launching a partnership that will power loans for customers of Western Union

Our big goal is to become the biggest bank in the world for friends and families who set their own terms with each other and are more inclined to pay each other. We are investing in behavioral science and, at critical mass, envision Zirtue becoming its own index to determine how healthy the market is. The data we are capturing is unique and very valuable to help us bring equality and transparency to access of capital for an underserved base of the population.

RON'S TAKE

There are some messy problems that well-established institutions simply won't touch. Lending between family and friends is one of those. And yet these loans represent both a massive addressable market and one riddled with challenges. Zirtue takes much of the agony, awkwardness, and unease out of the process. In fact, the elegance of the solution is that it solves multiple problems in one, including bill payment and the ability to help people get their credit back on a stronger footing.

From his own lived experience, Dennis can champion the solution to its target market of families who are low-income and frequently living paycheck to paycheck. Like the marketplace app offered by SoLo Funds, peer-to-peer lending is moving into a new age that will solve significant burdens faced by individuals who struggle to access capital in times of need.

POSSIBLE

Possible operates a platform for flexible short-term loans intended to aid individuals who are looking to build credit. The company's loans are designed to be simple and affordable, offered without a credit check, and allow for longer repayment schedules through multiple installments.

Headquarters and year founded: Seattle, 2017

Founder: Tony Huang founded Possible with the aim of making financial products fairer and more affordable for everyday people. Previously, Tony held several product and business development roles with Axon, a leader in connecting security devices. He has also been an elementary school teacher in the same school that he had attended as a youngster. Tony holds a degree in psychology from Harvard and has attended executive management programs at MIT and UC Berkeley.

Funds raised and VC investors: $156 million from Canvas Ventures, Euclidean Ventures, FJ Labs, Hustle Fund, Seattle Bank, Union Square Ventures, Unlock Venture Partners.

Q&A WITH THE FOUNDER

Where did the idea for Possible originate?

My co-founders and I didn't come from financial services or the lending business at all. We were building body cameras for cops and had spent cumulatively 26 years at Axon as part of their original software team. For the next stage in our careers, we wanted to have a big societal impact, and we thought a lot about how to help low-income minority communities through technology and data. At Axon, we would go into communities where there were no bank branches. It was just payday lenders everywhere. We thought there were a lot of pain points we could help solve in financial services for low-income communities. So, without experience, we dove right in. We turned down millions of dollars in offers of VC funding to pursue other ideas, but we wanted to go after this because the mission resonated with us. So, we ended up scraping together the first money, including from our former Axon boss, who wrote the first check.

What's the key problem that Possible intends to solve?

I liked the quote cited in your first blog post from *Poor Economics*, which says that poverty is not about a lack of money; it's the inability to live up to one's full potential. My family came from China. My Dad was at Tiananmen Square. Our family deeply cherishes the American ideal and, in many ways, we achieved the American dream of economic mobility for hard working people. However, we are seeing an erosion of mobility in the U.S., which is driving so much of the divisiveness in America today. There needs to be a better path to access financial services, capital, and credit that knocks people out of buying a home [or] car, renting an apartment, and achieving the American dream. We have customers who have been homeless and couldn't get an apartment simply because of having no credit score. We have a goal of unlocking economic mobility for many more Americans.

How are you most differentiated as a service?

When we first started Possible, we looked at payday loans. Should they even exist? The "first principles" answer is that credit should exist for low-income people. However, single payment products don't help build credit history. There is an incentive mismatch between lenders and consumers. Instead of onramps, payday loans were really debt traps. We wanted to create an onramp for low-income Americans buying offering small dollar loans with installment repay plans. This would allow borrowers to catch their breath and pay over multiple periods. Because it's an installment product, we focus on long-term financial health.

We took a lot of pains to get regulatory approval with federal and state lending laws to be a true credit provider to help our customers to build credit history. We didn't want a product that would lead to nowhere. We wanted to help lay the foundation for a brighter future.

What are the company's key accomplishments to date?

We have provided funds to around 600,000 unique individuals. We have issued 1.9 million loans to date, sometimes $50 or $100 at a time. I am proud of our team of 110 amazing individuals who work fully distributed from all parts of the U.S. and the globe.

What lies ahead for Possible?

We just announced a no-interest credit card product. We found that some of our customers were taking Possible loans repeatedly and we believe strongly in helping them graduate out of this predicament. Possible was supposed to be an onramp. Most customers do get off, but a small percentage are constantly coming back to borrow and remain stuck in a debt cycle. We were initially working to build a marketplace of consumer-friendly financial products. We got to know the credit card space from the outside and could see the misalignment of economic incentives that led to vicious debt cycles. So we decided to build our own credit card that would not charge any interest or penalties. We will be formally launching the Possible card later this year. After having announced the card in May, we already have 300,000 people on the waitlist. We intend to expand the total addressable market and also maintain the mission and ability to serve neglected low-income customers.

RON'S TAKE

Much like SoLo Funds and Zirtue, Possible is helping low-income individuals break the debt cycle and move away from reliance on usurious payday loans. Possible's unique value proposition is that its lending product establishes that critical onramp to building real credit that will allow borrowers to enter the economic mainstream of society and obtain traditional banking products and financial services. Tony Huang is a mission-driven founder who has demonstrated his ability to scale big ideas. As Possible launches new products in the months ahead, such as its no interest or fee credit card, it will be exciting to watch how many people are finally able to break the chains that hold them back from obtaining financial freedom.

PROPEL

Propel offers a mobile finance platform for low-income Americans to manage government benefits and debits side-by-side. The company's platform features the ability to view food stamps, locate grocery stores, corner stores, and farmer markets nearby instantly, as well as keep track of spending, enabling individuals with low income to improve their financial health, save money, find jobs, and earn income.

Headquarters and year founded: New York, 2014
Founder: Jimmy Chen founded and has served as CEO of Propel since 2014, having been compelled by a desire to bring technology to an important, overlooked segment of the population. Before this, Jimmy was a product manager at both LinkedIn and Facebook, as well as an intern at Yahoo and the World Bank. Jimmy is a graduate of Stanford University with a degree in symbolic systems.
Funds raised and VC investors: $90 million from Andreessen Horowitz, CLF Partners, Financial Solutions Lab, Financial Venture Studio, Flourish Ventures, Inspired Capital, JP Morgan Chase, Kleiner Perkins, Nyca Partners, Salesforce Ventures, SciFi VC, Serena Ventures, Thirtyfive Ventures.

Q&A WITH THE FOUNDER

Where did the idea for Propel originate?

I started Propel eight years ago through Blue Ridge Labs, which is part of the Robin Hood Foundation. I witnessed many of the challenges faced by low-income Americans. I was previously a Product Manager at Facebook and LinkedIn. I felt there was a better way for low-income people to navigate government benefits, which can often be bureaucratic and overly burdensome. I came to the United States from China at age four with my parents. I had a happy childhood, but money was always tight. My parents worked in restaurants and did odd jobs.

When I got to Stanford for college, I realized that there were people who came from very different financial backgrounds than I did. I got into coding, but one thing I realized early in my software career is that people tend to solve problems that they understand. Entrepreneurs and folks in venture capital tend to disproportionately come from wealth. To me, not focusing on problems of lower-income people was a huge, missed opportunity. In 2022, most people, including many of lower income, have smartphones and access to the Internet. Yet people in Silicon Valley are generally building apps for 25-year-old software engineers at Google. Not that many people are building software for single moms on food stamps in Kansas City.

What's the key problem that Propel intends to solve?

The concept for Propel is how to take what has been learned from top-tier tech companies like Facebook and apply this to the daily challenges of people living in poverty. In the summer of 2014, I spent most of my time talking to people in low-income households to gain insight into the challenges that they face, while thinking about those challenges that technology has the power to solve.

I started to learn about the social safety net. The food stamp program is used by 40 million Americans (one in eight residents). Benefits are provided via Electronic Benefits Transfer (EBT) debit cards issued by the state. However, the benefit recipient must call a 1-800-number on the back of the card just to find out what their balance is. Why isn't there a mobile banking app for this? I broadened this thinking into what else fintech can help solve.

We set out to make a product available to Americans in extreme financial need by building the country's first mobile banking app for the EBT card. Initially, this was a free app that showed balance and transaction history. We launched in early 2016 and got a lot of traction. For our customers, the experience should be no different than any other credit or debit card customer.

How are you most differentiated as a service?

We grew the user base rapidly through the first offering. As we talked to our customers we learned a lot about them. Government benefits are just one slice of their life. "Food stamps" are not a category or label for people. We wanted to address how to combine services that would help people make it through the month and therefore we extended to other offerings. We focus on how to help someone who is managing a family of four while earning a maximum of $28,000 per year.

We now serve 5 million monthly active users and are the most popular financial service product used by low-income Americans. We are extending into other services. Our debit card is built for customers who are earning under $40,000 per year and earning a government benefit. We help people to save money through household finance. We have partnerships with different retailers, both online and brick and mortar, through coupons. We work with utilities and telecoms like Comcast and T-Mobile. We also help users to earn more money by finding different types of work, both part and full-time. Last year over 300,000 people applied for jobs through us. Our customers define themselves as providers for families. Our aim is to help empower them to be good providers and provide services that they need.

What are the company's key accomplishments to date?

Our average monthly active user opens our app seventeen times per month. Our grocery coupons have saved our customers more than $60 million.

We conducted a study with Harvard Business School several years ago to find out how people used food stamps both before and with our app. With us, people were able to stretch their food stamps benefit by one day per month. That means an extra day of food per month for a low-income family that comes from average benefits of $250 per month. We help them to set a budget in a digital way that is convenient and modern. People can naturally set a budget that's more conducive to what they want.

In addition to this, we did a project with the GiveDirectly team to enable philanthropic contributions directly to our users. This was simply about raising money for direct cash payments to low-income Americans with us as the distribution channel. This was highly publicized, and we were able to serve $180 million through 180,000 cash grants. We believe this was the largest private cash transfer in American history. It's a simple way to send money to people in need with no cost or fees.

What lies ahead for Propel?

We plan to grow our digital banking product. Benefits aren't the entirety of our users' financial life. We plan to sit at the interaction of benefits and money by offering the opportunity for users to get income, including government benefits, which can be difficult to navigate and fully utilize. We are helping users get cash benefits that they probably qualify for but may not be able to access. We will become the core banking provider for low-income Americans.

We aim to become an institution like AARP but for low-income Americans. We will offer a platform with membership. We see AARP as a blueprint for what we can be with products tailored to this demographic and their multi-faceted financial lives.

RON'S TAKE

While it has been more than fifteen years since the late Professor C.K. Prahalad published *The Fortune at the Bottom of the Pyramid*, it is remarkable how few technology entrepreneurs have sought this market out by trying to truly understand the problems among those families and individuals who are at the lowest income rung of the ladder. This is precisely where Jimmy Chen received his motivation for building Propel into a platform leading in offering financial services and a community to support needs that many tech founders simply don't understand from not having had such a lived experience. The opportunity to solve problems are immense, and Propel, along with their backers, are well positioned to remain at the forefront of truly impactful product development.

ALTRO

Altro (formerly Perch Credit) operates an online credit-building platform designed to help users convert their subscription payments into credit history. The company's platform allows members to link recurring payments, such as rent and subscription payments, to leverage unseen and uncounted payments to build their credit scores, enabling individuals to upscale them.

Headquarters and year founded: Los Angeles, 2019

Founder: Michael Broughton is a social entrepreneur who is on a mission to break down barriers for the unbanked and those who lack credit. In addition to founding Altro (originally Perch) in 2019, Michael is vice chairman of the USC Credit Union (where, at 19, he was its youngest ever board member) and has been both a Thiel Fellow and a Sequoia Scout. He started Altro as a student at the University of Southern California.

Funds raised and VC investors: $18 million from Alumni Ventures, Backstage Capital, Black Capital, Citi Impact Fund (Citigroup Alternative Investments), Concrete Rose Capital, General Catalyst, Incite Ventures, Kapor Capital, Lombardstreet Ventures, Marcy Venture Partners, PayPal Holdings, Pendulum Holdings, Riverside Ventures, Sequoia Capital, Softbank Opportunity Fund, Think +, Underdog Labs, VentureSouq, Village Capital, Wonder Ventures, Y Combinator.

Q&A WITH THE FOUNDER

Where did the idea for Altro originate?

The idea started when I was entering college. I came from a family of nine people in one household on a single income. I was the first in my family to apply to a big institution like USC. I was fortunate enough to be accepted, but I couldn't come up with the tuition. I was $10,000 short. This led me to a situation where I couldn't start classes until I could figure this out.

I applied to private college student loan programs, but I was denied because I did not have personal financial credit. Our family finances didn't add up to what the lenders were looking for. I eventually figured it out by calling the university every day. However, I see the lack of accessibility that people like me face. I was thinking about what actionable steps I could take to help solve this. By my junior year at USC, I figured out what entrepreneurship was and began to think about how to solve this problem.

What's the key problem that Altro intends to solve?

It is a pretty clear problem. At least 68 million Americans reportedly lack access to a first financial product. They are stuck in a chicken-and-egg situation where they can't get credit without having a financial product (such as a bank account or credit card) and they can't get any product without having any credit. With Altro, we are simply working to lower this number. We want to show that there are more genuine creditworthy consumers in the market.

How are you most differentiated as a service?

Our platform is called Altro, which means "other" in French, and we are providing equitable access to credit for those who are being overlooked by the current system. We take things as simple as subscription payments to Netflix to help inform credit decisions. If consumers are paying this bill each month, they should be able to add to their credit lines. We help tie tradelines to one's Social Security number. This helps to both create and strengthen credit profiles.

Two things came together for us to make this work: Covid pushing the agenda for subscription services, and now being the first time that Wall Street and Capitol Hill are both lining up on the cause for equitable access. Wall Street wants to reach new customers, and Capitol Hill wants to fix the problem of access. We came in at the right time.

What are the company's key accomplishments to date?

We had a great year last year. Our app went viral under the original name, Perch Credit. Hundreds of videos have been recorded of people talking about it. We've had great community-led PR. We were Top 10 in the app store for more than a month. We then took a pause as we recognized this opportunity was greater than the six of us at USC could manage. We are now up to forty people. We have reset and rebuilt the app and have now rebranded it and are in the market with a true market fit. We have had 350,000 downloads to date.

What lies ahead for Altro?

There are still a lot of serious gaps in the credit agency model. People are scored on a 0–100 scale. Many consumers are between 40–70, which isn't a great score, and they need to work on it. A lot of financial products are available once you get past 60, such as credit cards, mortgages, etc. However, you don't see a lot offered to people who fall in the 0–40 range. We want to focus there. Many people can't get their first bank account. Big gaps exist for people who need that first product to set themselves up on a strong financial footing.

RON'S TAKE

Almost anyone would agree that the credit scoring system that lenders and financial services firms rely on is imperfect. However, for many people, it is downright broken and cruel, and there is little that individual consumers can do about it. A radical rethink is needed, particularly for those who are most financially vulnerable. Altro is bringing in new data points through everyday consumer purchases to help people establish and improve their credit. This will solve countless problems for millions of individuals while also opening opportunities for businesses to work with consumers that had been neglected and cast aside for far too long.

Disclaimer: Alumni Ventures invested in the Series A round of Altro in early 2022.

NED

Ned provides the rails and infrastructure so all types of capital lenders can serve small businesses in low-income and underserved communities.

Headquarters and year founded: New York, 2021
Founder: David Silverstein, founder and CEO, started Ned after serving as a senior executive in several large and mid-size media companies. Previously,

he was Press Secretary for former U.S. Senate Majority Leader Harry Reid. David is a graduate of Vanderbilt University and NYU Stern School of Business.

Funds raised and VC investors: $345,000 from Forum Ventures and angels.

Q&A WITH THE FOUNDER

Where did the idea for Ned originate?

The spirit for the business originated during my time working for Senator Harry Reid. It was a once-in-a-career opportunity to learn alongside brilliant people that worked relentlessly to strengthen communities across the country. There was an ethos on that team that we were part of a "good fight"—we fought for those that couldn't stick up for themselves. I've always wanted to help small business owners, and I'm building Ned with that spirit in mind.

About two years ago, I had a conversation with a friend, a small business owner in Brooklyn who is originally from Liberia. He had a hard time getting a loan. He needed to raise a small amount of money but didn't know how to go about it. This led me to start talking to lenders that are working in diverse communities. I discovered serious market friction whereby SMBs and lenders have a hard time coming together to make a fair and equitable deal.

What's the key problem that Ned intends to solve?

We are starting with lenders who've been left behind when it comes to technology. They need a way to move quicker, bring down costs, and assess risk when a basic credit score doesn't paint a full picture.

Specifically, there's a long tail of non-bank lenders, many of whom are nonprofit organizations or accept funding from the Treasury Department. These institutions typically have AUM of between $5–$150 million, and many lack the systems to do their job. They need affordable tech to help them manage the full lifecycle of a small business loan.

At Ned, we're building a set of rails to connect businesses and lenders in more fair and efficient ways. Our platform is an embedded operating system that gives lenders an affordable solution to underwrite business owners who have credit issues. Our software allows lenders to look quickly at business performance and assess creditworthiness based on the lender's own scoring criteria. We help approve and dispense loans by creating an infrastructure layer in the economy, which levels the playing field so lenders can do their job and disburse capital at speed.

How are you most differentiated as a service?

Our platform today offers revenue-based financing in a box, and we're building out capabilities so lenders can administer any debt product on our rails.

We worked with five design partners to create a central nervous system for their operation. Since we offer an all-in-one solution, we provide out-of-box integrations into Plaid, HelloSign, and Astra Finance (ACH). Our embedded portal takes care of applications, origination, and approval for lenders. Plaid integrations power loan qualification and a bespoke scoring system using the lender's own criteria. Integrated eSignature streamlines contracting, and we then automate disbursement and repayment. Ned drives the agreement from start to finish.

What are the company's key accomplishments to date?

We are in the process of going live with four of our design partners. The platform is working, customers are excited, and we will power our first real agreements in the coming weeks. We also have a top 20 U.S. bank starting paid pilots, in addition to the statewide and community lenders that we are working with. I'm proud that we're going to remove the friction around loan qualification that's prevalent for those lenders serving at the grassroots level or in low-income communities.

What lies ahead for Ned?

Historically, recessions last an average of ten months. Like other early-stage founders, I'm getting ready and raising money with the goal of building within the downturn to emerge stronger. Our business also has an economic tailwind as interest rates rise, and millions more business owners will have an even harder time finding money. We'll be there to provide technology so small lenders that serve low-income communities can get through a challenging set of quarters.

RON'S TAKE

The majority of the venture-backed fintech companies profiled in this book have been working directly on the front lines with borrowers and lenders facing challenges with a broken credit score system that exacerbates the wealth inequality problem. It is important to remember that there also needs to be a robust set of infrastructure players on the backend that will be there to support lenders who are serving lower-income borrowers and communities broadly. Ned is one such company that has taken on the less glamorous but vitally important work of enabling lenders to work with small business borrowers coming from a place where it is not easy to borrow in order to start or expand a business. If an increasing number of lenders are finally empowered to serve these overlooked communities, we will see more enterprises that benefit more people and increase overall wealth where it is needed the most.

SUNBIT

Sunbit builds financial technology that allows people to pay for services over time with ease. Their technology grants credit at more than 14,000 point-of-sale service locations in a matter of just moments to the majority of applicants, thereby removing the stress of paying for life's expenses by giving people more options on how and when they pay at U.S. auto dealership service centers, optical practices, thousands of dentist offices, veterinary clinics, and specialty healthcare services. Sunbit also offers a next-generation no-fee credit card that can be managed through a powerful mobile app.

Headquarters and year founded: Los Angeles, 2016
Founder: Arad Levertov, co-founder and CEO, started Sunbit in early 2016 after having been COO of Enova International, an $800 million fintech company with more than 1,000 employees that serves the needs

of non-prime consumers and small businesses. He was previously a systems developer at Intel and a Navy Seal in the Israel Defense Forces. Arad graduated in industrial engineering from Ben-Gurion University of the Negev (Israel) and received an MBA from the Fuqua School of Business at Duke University. His co-founders are Ornit Maizel (CTO), Tal Reisenfeld (head of sales) and Tamir Hazan (head of analytics).

Funds raised and VC investors: $210 million from AltaIR Capital, Alumni Ventures, Chicago Ventures, Group 11, G Squared, Heroic Ventures, Migdal Insurance, MORE Investment House, SkyDeck, Starting Line, Transpose Platform Management, Zeev Ventures.

Q&A WITH THE FOUNDER

Where did the idea for Sunbit originate?

Sunbit was born out of a combination of personal and professional experiences. Professionally, I had moved to the U.S. and started working in the fintech sector with a company that was serving the needs of people who lacked credit. I was also trying as an immigrant to build credit of my own.

After having been in the U.S. for two years, I applied for a store credit card at Costco. I talked to the cashier and provided her with all sorts of personal information that she requested. When the credit check came back, I was declined. It was embarrassing to both the cashier and to me. It turns out that 50 percent of point-of-sale credit applications get declined. At the time, I worked in a company that provides money upfront to people so that they could shop at places like Costco. I thought, why not just pay Costco directly, and eliminate the middleman? I connected the dots in my head—like the potential for cost savings for everyone involved—and saw the opportunity for what would become Sunbit.

My goal was to bring innovation, transparency, and personalization to the credit world, and turn the traditional business model of charging fees and the high interest rates on its head. And I wanted to be sure we served as many people as possible.

What's the key problem that Sunbit intends to solve?

Traditionally, companies are built primarily with profit in mind. My co-founders and I wanted to do something different: to create a drastically more customer-centric, personalized way for people to pay for everyday expenses, so that they could focus on the important things in life. Why shouldn't a company solve for the customer first?

We believed that if we brought value to everyone in our ecosystem—in our case, customers, service providers, and merchants—that the economic benefits would follow. One billion dollars in transactions later, that has proven to be true.

We are a fintech company for the real world, bridging the gap between things people need to pay for and the merchant's ability to give it to them while cutting out extraneous costs and fees. Sunbit started off meeting people where they were: where unexpected costs often emerged, like the auto parts and service shop, the dentist, the eye doctor. There, we were able to help customers when they needed it, with a point-of-sale solution offering quick credit approval, high approval rates, and the best personalized interest rates we can provide. Providers and merchants make the sale; everybody wins.

Our second product, the Sunbit Card, was created because we wanted to have more of an impact on more people; it's the next evolution of our commitment to customer experience. It is a new kind of no-fee credit card with a powerful mobile app that offers customers ultimate control and flexibility on how they want to pay for every single transaction they make, whether they want to pay it in full or over time. It helps simplify and centralize a lot of what we were hearing a lot of customers tell us they were managing in their heads—when to pay off what and how.

We have a Net Promoter Score of above 80. While you will not often see customers bragging on Instagram that they just fixed their brakes or had dental work done, the proof is in the numbers. Sunbit's there for customers when they need us.

How are you most differentiated as a service?

One key point of differentiation is on the credit side. There are some companies that lend money to prime credit customers and then there are others that focus on subprime customers, which are basically predatory lenders that charge hundreds of points or more in annualized interest rates. The latter type typically come in the form of payday loans and lease-to-own financing arrangements. In both cases, applications are arduous to fill out and often result in declines.

Our technology delivers experiences with the customer in mind. What we do is use technology that is ten times faster than applying for a credit card. We take just 30 seconds to have an answer and our point-of-sale product can approve nine out of ten applications. There simply isn't another financing technology that does that in-store. It's not only great for customers, but merchants love it and stick with us.

Likewise with the Sunbit Card, there are no late fees, no penalty fees, no membership fees, no application fees, and no fees to add or remove a transaction from a payment plan. Consumers get next-gen functionality at no cost beyond their personalized interest rate.

Sunbit believes that credit should work for everyone, everywhere – not just higher-income earners, who already have a lot of options.

What are the company's key accomplishments to date?

We started the company in 2016 and today offer our point-of-sale service in more than 14,000 locations, a figure that is currently growing by 600–700 per month. We have served over a million customers and completed more than $1 billion in transactions. We also have 70,000 customers who have already used the Sunbit Card and thousands more on the waiting list.

Our growth has been tremendous. This year, we were included in the top 10 percent of high-growth companies in the U.S. on the *Inc.* 5000 list. We also just became certified as a Most Loved Workplace®, with our employees reporting that they feel a sense of ownership and impact.

What lies ahead for Sunbit?

Sunbit has always built products that serve everyday Americans, and that's what you should expect to see from us in the future: more customer-centric, life-simplifying products that our customers depend upon.

Remarkably, 85 percent of merchant sales today of products and services are still brick and mortar and we will expand our offerings to meet the needs of both the customer and the merchant at the point of sale, in new and exciting markets.

In addition, I am excited about the future of the Sunbit Credit Card. We heard from our million-plus customers: they're managing many different transactions and forms of payment, all of which can make managing day-to-day finances tough. The Sunbit Card simplifies life by enabling all these types of transactions to be done on a single card.

Regardless of where we go with existing or new products, our underlying promise is to treat each customer or merchant like she was the only customer or merchant for Sunbit and to remember that there are real people behind the numbers.

RON'S TAKE

Life is full of unpleasant surprises, including unexpected bills for car repairs, dental work and countless other non-discretionary services. For those times, individuals of modest means and limited savings need to have options that work better than taking out a payday loan at usurious interest rates. Sunbit leverages technology to serve more people than traditional lending institutions and at better rates than what predatory lenders offer. In fact, Sunbit has become a "unicorn" company with a valuation exceeding $1 billion just by serving two of the many markets that exist with point-of-sale purchases. The opportunity to radically transform the access to affordable credit for unexpected expenses is becoming clear and for the taking.

Disclaimer: Alumni Ventures has invested in multiple financing stages of Sunbit, including most recently, the Series D round in mid-2021.

EMPOWER

Empower offers innovative credit and lending products to give more people a fair shot at getting money at a reasonable cost whenever they need it and boosting their credit history with every on-time payment. This enables greater financial, professional, and housing opportunities and a clear runway into the traditional credit system.

Headquarters and year founded: San Francisco, 2016

Founder: Warren Hogarth, co-founder and CEO, is an entrepreneur, investor, advisor, and board member at numerous early-stage technology companies. A former partner at the venture capital firm Sequoia Capital, Warren holds bachelor's and PhD degrees in chemical engineering from the University of Queensland (Australia) and an MBA from Harvard Business School.

Funds raised and VC investors: $60 million from Blisce, Defy Partners Management, Icon Partners, Initialized Capital Management, Launchpad Capital, Quiet Capital, Sequoia Capital, South Park Commons.

Q&A WITH THE FOUNDER

Where did the idea for Empower originate?

Empower originated based on my own experience of moving to the U.S. from Australia. I was fortunate in that I was financially literate, had a stable income, and was living within my means. I never needed credit and always paid my bills. Then it came time for me to get my first loan in order to buy a car. My credit application was rejected. I didn't understand as I was never late in paying my bills. I didn't realize that I needed to borrow money to pay bills in order to establish a credit rating. This was the genesis of the idea. Seven and a half years later, I was an experienced venture capital investor with Sequoia Capital. I saw some of the great fintech success stories firsthand, such as Stripe, Square, Nubank, and others. I saw an opportunity and had a unique window to solve the problem based on my experience and challenges in establishing credit.

What's the key problem that Empower intends to solve?

The primary problem is that 100 million people in the U.S. lack access to fair credit out of a population of 250 million consumers. These are people who either don't have a credit file or have made a mistake in the past. It is hard for many to get access to the financial system, and this is very important for gaining financial stability. It all goes back to Muhammad Yunus, who won the Nobel Peace Prize for Grameen Bank and providing microcredit. With 100 million people just in this country shut out of the financial system, Empower is working to solve this problem.

We offer instant cash flow based underwriting, something that is possible because of companies like Plaid. We have an automated savings piece. Our solution solves the problem for 50–60 percent of people who are shut out today. Our two core products are cash advances and lines of credit. For line-of-credit customers, credit reporting to all major bureaus provides an onramp to the financial system and helps people access and build credit.

How are you most differentiated as a service?

We do cash flow based underwriting. This is important for people who live paycheck to paycheck to gain an onramp. We build an automated repayment mechanism. This is tailored to those who are under financial pressure. We offer cash flow alongside a flexible payment plan for that customer to have the best chance of repaying on time and building positive credit history. We report to credit bureaus to provide an onramp back into the financial system.

What are the company's key accomplishments to date?

We have advanced over $500 million to borrowers to date and with this, have been able to demonstrate that the vast majority of people actually perform like prime users. We have seen low single digit default rates. In total, we have helped well more than one million people gain access to financial markets.

What lies ahead for Empower?

Our mission is to increase access to fair credit that enables social mobility. While we are helping to solve this in the U.S. market, the pain point is significantly higher elsewhere. We do not just want to be a service for the U.S. We want to help this issue globally.

RON'S TAKE

Accessing credit is something that is taken for granted by many, while not having credit is one of the biggest determinants of one's ability to become financially healthy and independent. Barriers have been erected by society over decades that must continue to be torn down if we want an economy and society that is truly inclusive. Empower is showing how solutions can scale rapidly that begin to make a dent in the problem. It helps everyone, including borrowers, lenders, merchants, and the public at large, if the playing field is leveled for everyone to access cash when needed and become part of the financial system.

2

CAPITAL AND CREDIT IN EMERGING ECONOMIES

I n the United States, as well as most industrialized nations, we take for granted the availability of capital and credit. Do you need a mortgage for a house you're buying? They're readily available, if not always affordable. Credit cards? We have more than we can use! Small business loans? The U.S. Small Business Administration helps small businesses get funding, and SBA-backed loans enable many small businesses to get the funding they need.

In developing nations, this is not always the case. The first problem is that billions of people are "unbanked"—that is, they have no relationship with any bank. Even in the United States, an estimated 4.5 percent of households (or 5.9 million) did not have anyone in the household with an account at a bank or with a credit union. If this sounds like a lot, consider that across the globe, an estimated 1.7 billion to 2.5 billion people are unbanked.

World Bank Group President Robert B. Zoellick said, "Providing financial services to the 2.5 billion people who are unbanked could boost economic growth and opportunity for the world's [impoverished]… Harnessing the power of financial services can really help people to pay for schooling, save for a home, or start a small business that can provide jobs for others."[11]

In Africa, which in the 21st century has seen some improvement in access to financial services, a significant proportion of the Sub-Saharan population remains unbanked. A report by the banking, payments, and commerce platform BPC revealed that 57 percent of Africans do not hold any kind of bank account, including mobile money accounts. "With a population of more than 1.1 billion people, Sub-Saharan Africa comprises a significant share of the global population while having the world's youngest overall population, with a median age of under 19 years."[12]

For many of these people, getting a loan—for any reason—is very difficult.

Traditionally, non-governmental organizations (NGOs) provided microfinance loans, typically between $20 and $300. Most NGOs were not registered as financial institutions, and typically depended on private donations for their lending funds. Then in 1976, the Grameen Bank in Bangladesh became the first private financial institution to extend microcredit on a large scale, and sought to demonstrate it was possible to extend loans to millions of poor people and still make a profit. In 1998, the bank's Low-Cost Housing Program won a World Habitat Award. Between 2003 and 2007, the bank grew significantly, and by January 2011, the bank's total number of borrowers had reached 8.4 million, with 97 percent being women. In 2006, the bank and its founder, Muhammad Yunus, were jointly awarded the Nobel Peace Prize.

As the World Bank noted in 2011, competition has emerged as the most important driver of financial innovation in Africa. "Expanding financial services to the unbanked [means] looking beyond existing institutions, products, and delivery channels, such as banks, traditional checking accounts, and brick-and-mortar branches. [Building a strong cultural foundation] means expanding financial literacy, developing consumer protections, and addressing constraints outside of the financial sphere, such as in agriculture."[13] Below are several venture-backed startups that are democratizing access to capital and credit in developing markets.

FIDO

Fido operates a digital financing platform designed to offer access to instant credit loans. The company's platform, which is currently in market in Ghana and expanding across Africa, offers credit to individuals without any fees, collateral, or guarantors, enabling users to have fast and easy access to funds.

Headquarters and year founded: Accra, Ghana, and Tel Aviv, Israel, 2013.

Founder: Its co-founder and president, Nadav Topolski, is an international entrepreneur with a passion for emerging markets and Africa in particular. He has worked extensively as a financial consultant in Africa and has also worked closely with his mentor Len Blavatnik of Access Industries, a major global investor in the media, telecommunications, chemicals, real estate and financial sectors. Nadav graduated in computer science and economics from the University of Haifa (Israel) and has an MBA from Harvard Business School.

In addition, Fido's CEO Alon Eitan joined the company in mid-2021 after having led strategy and corporate development at Guesty, a leading hospitality software platform. Alon has also worked in venture capital and M&A at Clal Industries and as a valuation and strategy advisor with PwC. He holds degrees in finance, accounting and economics from the Hebrew University of Jerusalem and Tel Aviv University.

Funds raised and VC investors: The company has raised and total $38 million from Alumni Ventures, Fortissimo Capital, and angel investors.

Q&A WITH THE FOUNDER

Where did the idea for Fido originate?

The idea originated a few years ago when Tomer, Nir, and I, old friends from Haifa, were working in different capacities in Africa and wanted to find an interesting problem to solve together. I was then reading the book *Poor Economics* by Esther Duflo and Abhijit Banerjee, both professors of economics at MIT and Nobel Memorial Prize in Economic Sciences laureates. The book discusses the problem of the lack of access to financing as one of the main obstacles for growth in poor economics. This became the problem we were and are still excited to solve.

What's the key problem that Fido intends to solve?

Lack of access to financial services is a key constraint on the growth of entrepreneurship in Africa. The banking sector is complicated and bureaucratic, its processes are time-consuming and not really customer-friendly, so access to financial services remains beyond the reach of a significant segment of the population.

How are you most differentiated as a service?

Fido changes this paradigm by automating the whole customer journey from onboarding to credit analysis and even provides financial guidance. Our autonomous banking platform and unique machine learning risk models make instant credit decisions even for customers with no financial track record while helping reduce operational costs.

Fido's autonomous banking system relies on mission-critical, real-time machine learning models for risk scoring and fraud detection, based on non-financial data, to approve or reject a loan in real time, and simultaneously deliver market-leading default rates. The B2C mobile application is fast, data-driven, low latency, and built on a distributed cloud architecture, helping boost accessibility to financial services to unbanked regions.

We are going beyond just digital financial services and aim to educate customers on how to improve their credit scores over time and incentivize positive financial behavior. Later this year, we plan to launch savings and cost-effective payment products in some of its markets to help users easily improve their financial health with a product that's simple to use.

What are the company's key accomplishments to date?

The company has grown to a team of sixty that includes data scientists, engineers, and financiers, while already having underwritten 1.5 million loans to more than 340,000 customers at a value of over $150 million. Moreover, Fido was just named the #1 app in the Ghana Play Store!

What lies ahead for Fido?

We are planning to launch new financial products in Ghana, such as savings and payments; grow our customer base across Africa; and establish a tech center in Accra to train engineers for higher levels of software development. We are building a new culture of money in Africa by making financial services instant and accessible.

RON'S TAKE

Fido's strategy of providing credit and banking services to the unbanked gets right to the heart of solving one of the biggest problems that people living in emerging economies face.

Traditional banks and other financial institutions have proven unable or unwilling to accept the risk of working with small individual customers who come from modest financial means. This is the chicken-and-egg problem that Fido and other neobanking companies like them are working to solve. In Fido's case, this is being done by leveraging machine learning technology that has been previously untapped in order to grow the market of borrowers and operate efficiently at scale. As Fido expands in Ghana and soon launches into other sub-Saharan Africa nations, the continent is sure to rise as more and more people are empowered to achieve their goals.

Disclaimer: Alumni Ventures invested in the Series A round of Fido in June 2022.

CARBON

Initially focused in Nigeria, Carbon provides short-term loan services intended to empower all people with financial access. The company's platform empowers individuals with access to credit, simple payment solutions, high-yield investment opportunities, and easy-to-use tools for personal financial management.

Headquarters and year founded: Lagos, Nigeria, 2012
Founder: Chijioke Dozie is a serial entrepreneur and investor across multiple industries. He worked as an investment professional with Zephyr Management and the International Finance Corporation (IFC) before starting Kaizen Venture Partners, which incubated the concept that turned

into Carbon. A native of Nigeria, Chijioke studied economics and finance at the University of East Anglia and the University of Reading in the U.K., and he holds an MBA from Harvard Business School.

Funds raised and VC investors: $13 million from Google for Startups, Kaizen Venture Partners, Net 1 UEPS Technologies (now Lesaka).

Q&A WITH THE FOUNDER

Where did the idea for Carbon originate?

I have worked in private equity with Zephyr Management, as well as for the IFC, covering many sectors, including agriculture and manufacturing in Africa. In these roles, I ran into opportunities in consumer finance that were not being adequately addressed, such as the need for extending credit to people, from those working in mines to teachers. In Nigeria, we have a big issue with a lack of access to credit for most people as banks simply were not tackling this. My father founded a bank, and I know where the dead bodies are. Most bankers see retail deposits as a means to end. Their real business is to give loans to corporations and buy T-bills (treasury bills). I enrolled for my MBA at Harvard Business School with this challenge in mind as the key problem that I wanted to tackle.

Post-HBS, I started my company Kaizen. We picked several countries in sub-Saharan Africa where there was a gap in the consumer credit market. We raised funding from the IFC and explored multiple investment opportunities. Out of this grew Carbon, which was a huge opportunity and we decided to focus on this business. Nigeria is a huge country of more than 200 million people, of which only 14 million even have bank accounts. Only 50 million people have a debit card, and a meager 300,000 people hold a credit card. The ratio of credit to GDP is just 6 percent. Almost no one has access to credit.

We started a bank debt collection business in order to better understand the problem and opportunity. We learned that banks were doing a bad job not only of issuing loans but in collections as well. Secondly, customers wanted to pay but often couldn't simply because banks froze their accounts. I also did a little test by calling the bank that Father had started, requesting a $2,000 personal loan. Now, mind you, I had a business with the bank that was pulling in $17,000 in cash flow per day. It took four weeks to get back to him, and they finally said that I needed to provide a personal guarantee. I have been able to get credit facilities while living in several foreign countries without even having a job, but I couldn't get a loan from a bank in my home country that already knew me well.

What's the key problem that Carbon intends to solve?

We started off as a consumer lender. In 2015, we raised a Series A from NASDAQ-listed company NetOne. However, we realized we couldn't beat banks at their own game without having a branch distribution network or substantial capital. We didn't have a customer base, so we pivoted to creating a digital app that would allow loans to anyone around the country who had a cell phone. We got 8,000 new applications per day. It was an exciting but scary experience. We couldn't meet our customers in person, verify payslips, etc. New payment processors were coming into the market that could tokenize debit cards and pull repayments on a schedule. A user could log in, enter debit card details, go through verification, then tokenize to agree to a direct debit schedule. This was the catalyst that enabled our leap into the digital space. We did this successfully for three years and then started adding other services. There is still a large market for better and cheaper products versus traditional banks. We offer a savings product with higher interest rates; we allow customers to pay cable, phone, and utility bills without charging convenience fees; and we don't charge for checking accounts, peer-to-peer transfers, or other services.

How are you most differentiated as a service?

Our vision is to be a digital bank for Africans and the diaspora. We enable customers to have friction-free experiences, and we want to be everywhere for customers. A Carbon account should act like a passport that works across borders. Want to enable customers in more ways than a typical financial institution, including insurance. There is now a proliferation of neobanks in Africa, and it's getting very hard to distinguish each one from the other. All have "free" everything. We differentiate with our buy now, pay later (BNPL) offering of zero percent financing for up to six months. For example, our customers can pay any school fees without a premium. This is a unique selling point.

What are the company's key accomplishments to date?

We have over three million registered customers and are gaining over 70,000 new each day. Our app has had over two million downloads, and revenue is over $1 million a month. Even when we were purely a digital lender, we had an 80 percent repeat rate and a 12 times LTV:CAC (lifetime value to customer acquisition cost) ratio.

What does the future hold for Carbon?

We are really going to focus on the BNPL opportunity. We have looked at the broad sub-Saharan retail banking opportunity. The retail market in Nigeria accounted for $150 billion spent in 2019, of which $27 billion was non-essential retail. This market is mostly cash-based and virtually untouched by credit. There is a huge opportunity in Nigeria alone and we want to capture a significant portion of that. We plan to become the biggest retail finance institution in the country. Our long-term goal is to extend this into other markets. People transact every day. We plan to embed BNPL, and then ultimately also move into issuing credit cards.

RON'S TAKE

The opportunity to democratize access to capital and credit is fundamental to empowering individuals across the world, but the problem is particularly acute in particular markets where banks have proven to be high-risk and innovation-averse. Carbon is breaking down barriers in the most populous African country, Nigeria. With founder and CEO Chijioke Dozie's background in international financial markets, banking, and technology, he has the vision to deliver what consumers need. Numerous fintech and neobank companies across Africa are tackling these problems. It will be exciting to watch over the coming years as hundreds of millions of individuals are empowered to earn, spend, and live their full lives without the historically unbreakable barriers on how much capital they are able to access in times of need.

FINICS

FINICS operates a buy now, pay later (BNPL) platform that enables individuals in Mexico to afford healthcare services whenever they are needed.

Headquarters and year founded: Mexico City, 2022
Founder: Nico Maffey, co-founder and CEO, has had a career spanning the government, academia, nonprofit, and financial services sectors. Most recently, he was a Public Leadership Fellow at Harvard University and a digital development consultant at the World Bank. A native of Argentina, Nico is a graduate of Harvard College and holds an MPA in International Development from the Harvard Kennedy School.
Funds raised and VC investors: Under $1 million from Allston Venture Fund and angels.

Q&A WITH THE FOUNDER

Where did the idea for FINICS originate?

While working toward my MPA in International Development, I decided that I wanted to start a consumer fintech company in Latin America and Mexico specifically. I knew that the market was dominated by traditional retail banks that charge high interest rates, have restrictive access to banking products, etc. Through my program at the Harvard Kennedy School, I met my initial co-founder Ana Alvarez, who comes from Mexico and shared the same idea.

We initially set out to create the Credit Karma or Lending Tree for LatAm. We would match borrowers with the best lender available. After pursuing this for some time, we realized that the unit economics of these businesses would take a long time to take off. We got to understand a lot about borrowers in Mexico, however, and we found out that 15 percent of personal loans were for medical services. Many people cannot afford unexpected medical expenses, and most personal loans can take up to two months to get processed by traditional banks and lenders. We decided to go after this market with FINICS and received some initial funding and acceleration from the Allston Venture Fund, Harvard i-lab, MassChallenge, MIT Sandbox, and angel investors. We also won non-dilutive funding through the MIT Social Enterprise competition.

What's the key problem that FINICS intends to solve?

FINICS is built to solve the problem of people in Mexico who cannot afford healthcare services. Less than 10 percent of people have private health insurance, and almost 70 percent rely on the public health system. Insurance is expensive, and there is a cultural aversion to it. This results in 55 percent of medical expenses for Mexicans being paid out of pocket. We decided to bring to market a BNPL solution for medical loans, which is novel to this market. This would benefit both the patients and the medical providers. A significant portion of the population is denied medical attention because they cannot afford it, and it simply takes too long for someone to get approved for a loan when timing is of the essence.

Our solution offers competitive loans and fast pre-approval in less than a minute at the point of sale. We have our own credit scoring system that does not exclusively require information from credit bureaus since fewer than half of Mexicans even have a credit score. Instead, we work with medical providers to collect information such as earnings, where people live, and the type of intervention needed, and we can use this information to provide a decision on the spot. For the provider, our value is in eliminating awkward conversations on financing with patients, suring up revenue, and increasing conversion rates.

How are you most differentiated as a service?

The two main alternatives available in the healthcare space in Mexico are credit cards and personal loans. What's different about FINICS is that we can work directly with providers and patients to make decisions. Credit cards in Mexico have less than 25 percent penetration, and loans take a long time and are not compatible with medical needs. Banks don't have integrations with hospitals and medical providers, but we do. We are able to reduce risk and offer more competitive rates.

What are the company's key accomplishments to date?

We started to pilot with a few medical providers. This is going well, and we are now partnering with a large hospital in Mexico City. The first big deals are now coming in while we refine the credit scoring model. It's currently a difficult market context for BNPL, especially in emerging markets, but we are very happy with the traction so far and see a significant demand for our solution.

What lies ahead for FINICS?

We are going to embark on further fundraising while we stay lean. Despite the economic recession, medical expenses are not cyclical. As interest rates rise, customers are having a harder time finding financing. We aim to create a frictionless experience to help Mexicans interact with the medical system.

RON'S TAKE

This chapter has looked at BNPL companies in different sectors and geographies. They all boil down to enabling those with limited financial resources to obtain services that are needed in a quick and painless manner. Arguably no services are more critical than receiving healthcare. It is an indictment on societies broadly when basic health services cannot be met simply because a patient does not have the means to pay for it. This issue is particularly acute in emerging economies, including Mexico, where FINICS is attempting to disrupt the old way of doing things that ends up failing so many. Ensuring the ability to obtain healthcare at the moment it is needed will save lives and provide comfort for those who do not have sufficient personal savings to cover whatever unexpected events come their way.

Disclaimer: Nico Maffey served as venture fellow with Alumni Ventures in 2022.

EMTECH

Emtech provides a cloud-based software designed to provide central banks in emerging markets with scalable and resilient digital infrastructure.

Headquarters and year founded: New York, 2019

Founder: Carmelle Cadet, founder and CEO, is a mission-driven founder who brings to Emtech more than ten years of experience at IBM, where she was a leader in blockchain, financial services, and risk management. Carmelle holds a bachelor's in finance from Florida Atlantic University and an Executive MBA from NYU's Stern School of Business.

Funds raised and VC investors: $4 million from 500 Global, Canaan Partners, Consonance Investment Managers, Gilgamesh Ventures, LoftyInc Capital Management, NetX, NOEMIS Ventures, Octerra Capital, XFactor Ventures.

Q&A WITH THE FOUNDER

Where did the idea for Emtech originate?

I was born in Haiti and moved to the U.S. as a teenager. My family was unbanked when we arrived here, and I became interested in how technology and financial services could help solve challenges in emerging countries and low-income groups. Most of my career prior to Emtech was spent at IBM, where I helped to build an enterprise software business from nothing to $100 million of annual recurring revenue (ARR). I then left to work as deputy CFO of the Blockchain division. This is where I had my lightbulb moment to create better financial markets. I wanted to build a platform that would leverage blockchain technology to digitize cash and solve the problem of financial inclusion. After having done a project for the Central Bank of the Bahamas, I decided to take that experience and apply it to developing next-generation modern banking for central banks in Africa, where I saw the greatest opportunity.

What's the key problem that Emtech intends to solve?

We have taken a platform approach to designing a SaaS solution that allows central banks to have API access to retail banks and fintech companies, such as fully digital neobanks, that would help de-risk financial services.

How are you most differentiated as a service?

We build modern infrastructure that sits between these institutions and utilizes modern financial infrastructure. Emtech provides a cloud SaaS model that is modern, more efficient, and charges a simple license fee to central banks with API call fees to users. Our focus is West Africa, where we have signed three central banks and are in talks with six more. Our platform provides currency exchange and digital compliance services, all-in-one. It is built for multi-country exchange. Banks can't close the gaps for financial inclusion all on their own. They don't have the KYC and regulatory frameworks in place to work in the fintech sandbox with digital currency.

What are the company's key accomplishments to date?

Emtech's platform has gone live with the Bank of Ghana through a multi-year SaaS agreement. We are also busy rolling out in Nigeria and Liberia. We are also helping fintechs and working with accelerator hubs. Our solution helps fintech get to market faster.

What lies ahead for Emtech?

We expect to have six countries converting over the coming months, which will get us to $100M ARR within 3–5 years. We will launch a multi-central banks strategy in collaboration with several partners, including Visa. Longer term, we also plan to enter the U.S. market, which presents its own challenges and opportunities.

RON'S TAKE

The institutional and regulatory barriers to offering credit and capital to all are in the midst of a massive disruption. This is thanks in large part to the neobanks and other fintech companies leveraging digital technologies such as AI, machine learning, and blockchain to tackle these challenges.

The chicken-and-egg problem of people not being able to borrow because they don't have credit history is a solvable one when intelligent systems are brought into play. The capital sources that begin with a country's central bank institutions must be ready and adaptable to meet these challenges. This requires the kind of infrastructure layers that Emtech is providing. Having already signed licensing agreements with several central banks of Africa, we can expect to see Emtech empowering millions more across the world who seek personal and small business loans over the years to come.

3

FINANCIAL WELLNESS AND EDUCATION

Basic financial literacy is regrettably not taught in all of our nation's high schools. A student can graduate with an advanced knowledge of trigonometry, fluency in a foreign language, and a working grasp of chemistry and physics, and know nothing about how credit card interest is compounded or how to budget for one's cost of living.

Are kids learning about personal finance at home? The answer is "no." Research suggests parents are nearly as uncomfortable talking to their children about sex as they are about money! A 2017 T. Rowe Price Survey revealed that 69 percent of parents hesitate to discuss financial matters with their kids. Only 23 percent of kids surveyed said they talked about money with their parents, and 35 percent said their parents were uncomfortable when it came to the subject of money.[14]

When American 15-year-olds were tested on their financial literacy, they ranked 7th out of fifteen countries, behind China, Canada, Russia, and Australia. The study by the Organisation for Economic Co-operation and Development (OECD) noted that for many 15-year-olds, finance is part of everyday life. They are already consumers of financial services such as bank accounts, and they earn money from formal or informal small jobs. As they near graduation, they "face complex and challenging financial choices, including whether to continue with formal education and, if so, how to finance such study".[15]

The lack of personal finance education in this country is a serious problem. It has led many people—not just young adults, but people of all ages—to rack up credit card and student loan debt, live paycheck to paycheck, and not save enough for retirement. It can hinder being able to buy a home or even pay rent, make car payments, or cover unexpected medical bills.

The problem is worse for children of color. Black families have struggled for decades to build wealth in America. Historical injustices, including slavery, systematic inequality, employment discrimination, and racist housing policies, have stifled the ability of Black families to reach parity with white families. Closing the racial wealth gap in the U.S. is complicated, but expanding financial literacy, education, and job training efforts are vital in this effort.

According to the 2022 TIAA Institute-GFLEC Personal Finance Index, Black Americans correctly answered an average of 37 percent of the study's financial literacy questions, whereas white Americans correctly answered an average of 55 percent. As Annuity.org reported, insurance knowledge tends to be particularly weak among Black people, followed closely by comprehending risk, investing, and identifying reliable sources of financial information.[16]

Here are three early-stage tech companies that are dedicated to expanding financial wellness and education, particularly for people of color who are employees of companies.

OFCOLOR

OfColor offers a financial wellness platform designed to improve the financial health of employees of color. The company partners both directly with employers as well as HR benefit providers to offer their clients' employees wealth-building solutions focused on budgeting, savings, and automated debt reduction, thus enabling employers to save on benefits, improve retention and compel recruitment while improving the financial health of minority employees.

Headquarters and year founded: Maplewood, NJ, 2019
Founder: Yemi Rose is the founder and CEO of OfColor. Yemi has spent nearly
    twenty years at the intersection of financial services and communications/

marketing focused on financial wellness, most recently as the vice president of Financial Wellness Enterprise Initiatives with Prudential Financial's Global Communications Group. He led the development of Prudential's Financial Wellness Census research project, as well as "The Cut," which focused on underserved consumers. He writes and speaks extensively on the racial wealth gap, and his writings on the subject have been published in *Time*, *Black Enterprise*, *The Root*, Blavity, BenefitsPro, and Money.com. Yemi has also previously worked with major financial institutions such as BlackRock, KPMG, and Thomson Financial. He holds both bachelor's and master's degrees in communications from Cornell University.

Funds raised and VC investors: $2.7 million from PSG and Techstars.

Q&A WITH THE FOUNDER

Where did the idea for OfColor originate?

I came up professionally through several large financial services companies, starting in the analyst training program at Thomson Financial. I have long been working at the intersection of finance and communications, which is my academic background. I have also been on a personal journey as an immigrant and have been amazed at how this country tolerates such a huge racial wealth gap. I lost a sister to suicide in 2013, and the key thing that came up after her death was the massive amount of short-term debt that she owed and the creditors who came after my mom, my other sister, and me. I came to a moment in life where I decided to *lean in* on purpose. At BlackRock, I was part of a massive machine and did not feel like I was making a real impact. Prudential offered me the opportunity to lean in on purpose as the leader of their financial wellness census, which was especially targeting underserved groups. There, I had a front row seat to financial wellness.

Through this experience, I knew that I wanted to focus on the folks most in need of intervention, namely employees of color. These are the folks most impacted by the racial wealth gap. I thought to myself whether to stick around and build something there at Prudential or to leave and try to do it on my own. I chose the latter and originally didn't know what part of the myriad of tools to tackle first. The wealth gap is so large that it can be really disheartening. But then I really looked into the data, and leaned in. I tested a few "silver bullet" ideas at first, and finally came ultimately to a vision of creating a holistic tool set that meets people where they are.

What's the key problem that OfColor intends to solve?

Putting a real dent in the racial wealth gap is the north star for our entire team, but we know that we are only tackling a small slice of the problem right now. This is because we're focused on people who already have jobs, and good ones with benefits at that. But it's a start for us and we make sure that we continue to advocate for policy change while we also do our work. We come to work every day focused on empowering workers of color to build wealth by giving them the technology, content, coaching, and community. There are a lot of large employers out there that want to live their values and support minority employees but may not know where to start. Anti-bias training can only go so far, and token promotions don't solve the underlying issues. We offer an alternative that focuses on all employees of color and looks to drive real change in their lives.

The tools and resources of personal finance default "white," meaning tools aren't built with people who look like me in mind. They tend to ignore systemic barriers to wealth creation. We leaned into the language and how we talk about problems and issues. This all crafted how the platform looks. People of color are at the center. We provide tools for budgeting, savings, financial literacy, and content that recognizes the minority money experience.

How are you most differentiated as a service?

The personal finance industry very often ignores the systemic barriers to wealth creation. We flip all of this on its head. We have built a financial services platform for us, by us, that puts people of color at the center. We provide users with financial advice from coaches who look like them and can help to guide them through. We deploy in enterprises and focus on driving engagement. We are driving true systemic changes. Our platform helps organizations as well by reducing costs such as payroll taxes and healthcare spending and by increasing productivity. Our value to the individual is to help them build out a financial legacy.

What OfColor offers is not very easy to replicate. As one of very few Black founders who have raised this type of funding, we have an opportunity to lean in and create a company that will be built for us by us. Many real changes are happening at scale, and companies are coming to us realizing that what we have built is special and unique.

What are the company's key accomplishments to date?

While we are just in our early days, we have already signed agreements and deployment with leading employers such as CVS. We came up through their Techstars accelerator program. To support their efforts to improve the financial health of all employees nationally, we work to drive content with their client partners and ensure minority money perspectives are represented.

What lies ahead for OfColor?

Driving real change is difficult work, and so we are focused on really building up the community-focused aspects of our offering that will serve to drive engagement with our offering. We aim to both entertain and increase knowledge that leads to financial health and legacy. This year look for us to continue to enhance our community and social platform offerings, as well as IP that offers fair capital to users that need it. In our first year of deployment, we are engaging with employee resource groups. We aim to both entertain and increase knowledge that leads to financial health and legacy.

We believe the workplace is one of the frontlines in the battle to close the racial wealth gap. If we improve the financial health of the employees that are most in need of help (known to be employees of color), then we create a ripple effect that benefits their companies and communities. Our goal is to grow the platform and usership to a point where users have a single place to get their money right, learn how to navigate biases in our financial system, and can actually invest towards building a financial legacy. Put simply, we intend to create a real ripple effect by driving systemic change.

While segments of the country are pushing back on talking openly about the barriers and burdens that have been placed systemically on racial minorities in the U.S., the need is becoming increasingly acute to chip away at these barriers and the inequities they have created. Specifically, the way personal finance institutions speak to Black and other communities of color needs to change. Yemi Rose's deep experience in financial communication and his passion for impact will give OfColor a sustainable edge as they partner with organizations that understand that better financial tools and a more customized experience will lead to more engagement, financial literacy, and well-being across the board. OfColor is still at a nascent stage but has tapped into an opportunity of enormous magnitude to correct wrongs and build more wealth equality from the bottom up.

BRIGHTUP

BrightUp operates a financial wellness platform intended to democratize financial wealth building and personal well-being. The company's platform partners with employers to deliver a comprehensive financial wellness benefit to their employees to grow their net worth and improve their self-worth. It also offers low-cost emergency loans that are repaid through paycheck deductions, enabling employees to be financially healthy and holistically wealthy.

Headquarters and year founded: Boston, 2020

Founder: Valerie Mosley, founder and CEO, previously created Valmo Ventures to advise and invest in companies that add value both to investors and society. She has invested in and advised Fundify (a platform for connecting startups and investors), Quantum Exchange (maker of the first quantum computer in the U.S.), STEAMRole (a career networking platform), tEQuitable (a confidential platform to address harassment at workplaces), and more. She also serves on the boards of DraftKings, Eaton Vance's Family of Mutual Funds, Dynex, NY Common Fund's Investment Advisory Committee, and Progress Investment Management

Company. Valerie is a graduate of Duke University and holds an MBA from the Wharton School of Business.

VC Investor: Kapor Capital.

Q&A WITH THE FOUNDER

Where did the idea for BrightUp originate?

The story of BrightUp originates with a couple of personal stories from my family. While I have enjoyed a very successful career as an executive and board member in the financial sector and asset management with prominent organizations such as Wellington, my late older brother turned out to have lived his entire life unbanked. I would have to occasionally lend him money to help him out and I always needed to send it via Western Union. I couldn't understand why I had to spend such high transfer fees compared to making a transfer through a bank.

Meanwhile, my sister, who works as a nurse, took out a car loan a few years ago and was offered by the dealer to finance the car at a 13 percent APR, which felt outrageous to me. I stepped in to negotiate on her behalf and was able to talk them down to 9 percent.

There is a report from the Federal Reserve called "The Color of Wealth" that found that the average net worth of a white family in America is $147,000, while the same for a Black family was $8. Yes, just *eight dollars*. This kind of financial stress takes a toll on people. At BrightUp, we believe that all people deserve to be financially healthy and holistically wealthy. That is our motto.

What's the key problem that BrightUp intends to solve?

The wealth management industry focuses on people who have assets because that's how they get paid. I grew up in inner-city Philadelphia from age five to twelve. When my father came out of the service and entered the private sector, he was given stock options that turned out to go up in value enough that we were able to move into a different neighborhood that had houses surrounded by grass. This opened my eyes to a different world. I want to make sure that more people get access to information, tools, and technology that allows them that goal of financial health and holistic wealth.

How are you most differentiated as a service?

We focus on creating a trinity of services through our platform that covers capital, content, and coaching:

- Capital that is available to refinance high-cost debt through an algorithm that disrupts the FICO score that is profoundly unfair and non-predictive of loan repayment ability. FICO credit scores explain only 6 percent of defaults. We offer an alternative pricing structure that looks at 150 different factors to establish creditworthiness.
- Content that is relatable as better and clear information is one of the top requests that employees have as a work benefit.
- Coaching to help people understand their financial picture and what strategies to take for their personal long-term objectives.

We partner with employers as well as offer our services directly to consumers.

What are the company's key accomplishments to date?

We have developed a minimally viable product (MVP), we have our first customer in the city of Columbia, South Carolina, and we have developed an emergency loan offering that does not rely on a FICO credit score. Our platform's employee adoption rate with our first customer is already 2.5 times what the benefits director expected.

What lies ahead for BrightUp?

We plan on growing from offering emergency loans to full debt consolidation. We will offer a greater suite of content that will meet end users where they are. There will be a set of articles and information behind a paywall. We also plan to develop an asynchronous course of financial well-being. Everyone comes with their own problems, and we want to help solve these in a thoughtful way through our trinity of capital, coaching, and content.

Why is it that only wealthy people should get access to strategies that help them to become financially healthy? It shouldn't be like this. With technology, tools, and compassion, we can solve this. We want to disrupt the wealth management industry by serving those communities that have been underserved or not served at all for far too long.

RON'S TAKE

Much like OfColor, BrightUp is bringing an important arsenal to the mix of employee benefits that will have a meaningful role in bringing financial literacy and wellness to a broader, overlooked audience. Valerie has an impressive background as a financial services professional, which combined with her personal family history, lends itself to understanding the needs of the communities that BrightUp will serve. Financial wellness tools are likely to become a staple of employer benefits, and these are two of the organizations that are innovating with the right content and offerings at the right time.

STACKWELL

Stackwell is an early stage fintech startup empowering a new community of Black investors. Its mobile application, to be launched publicly in spring 2022, delivers automated tools and education to help Black Americans stack and build wealth.

Headquarters and year founded: Boston, 2021
Founder: Trevor Rozier-Byrd, founder and CEO. Originally from New Jersey, Trevor moved to Boston to attend Boston College and later Boston University law school. He became a corporate transaction lawyer in New York with Sidley Austin, working on securities, fund management, private equity, hedge funds, and related financial services. Returning to Boston, Trevor moved into M&A and venture capital law with WilmerHale. He ultimately transitioned to in-house counsel and then management roles at State Street Bank, where he pivoted to strategy and business development.

Trevor rose to Managing Director at State Street before deciding to pursue his passion, leading to Stackwell Capital.

Funds raised and VC investors: $5.6 million from CMFG Ventures, Financial Health Network, Shea Ventures, SSC Venture Partners, The Kraft Family Foundation, and angel investors.

Q&A WITH THE FOUNDER

Where did the idea for Stackwell originate?

There were two main catalysts for me to start Stackwell. I was at a point in my career where I was ready to take the next step in my leadership journey. I wanted to have a broader impact on the community as I was always the only Black person or only Black male in the room. This comes with a strong sense of desire and obligation to give back to people who look like me.

In considering what to do next, issues of the racial wealth gap were top of mind. We have a ton of information on the stock market and how powerful it can be for creating wealth. There is also no gatekeeper to accessing the financial markets as there is in many other areas, such as qualifying for a loan. No one can tell someone else that they can't come in and participate in the financial markets. No one can limit someone's ability to gain the same return as anyone else. The stock market is within everyone's reach. I want to give more people in the Black community access to investment products and information, which will have positive ripple effects in the Black community. These are long-term social and economic benefits.

How does Stackwell's offering work?

In phase one, we are delivering a robo-investing product. We create model investment portfolios that take the mystery and fear out of the investing process. By leveraging principles of behavioral sciences, we empower a user's development. We create and sustain a path for our users to ultimately achieve their long-term financial goals and objectives. We leverage the experience of everyone on our team to do this.

In terms of how it works, a user signs up for the app, we ask a series of questions around the user's risk profile and investment horizon. We run algorithms that then suggest which portfolio is best suited to that user. Our portfolios are based on broad-based index ETFs, covering both equities and fixed income. We help align our users to the appropriate asset class. We are focused on delivering a model investment portfolio. Stackwell's automated solution helps people get into the market and takes stress out of the process of selecting stocks. It is not about trying to buy low and sell high. We take a broad-based and diversified approach.

What differentiates the product?

We have created a simple and easy-to-use product and delivered it with an accessible price point of just $1 a month and only a $10 investment minimum. Our goal is to help promote greater inclusion across the income spectrum. We want to break down barrier of why people don't invest in the market. Many people feel that it requires a lot of money to participate or don't know where or how to start to invest for themselves or their family. By reducing barriers, we try to take out the angst and anxiety.

How does this product specifically fit the Black community?

Everything we are doing is architected toward social, emotional, and cultural barriers that exist in the Black community. We aim to communicate directly with this user base by using language and imagery that will resonate and increase comfort and confidence in the process. We wrap everything into delivering a product and technology experience that works with our community. There is a lack of confidence in investing because we are not having the right conversations. How do we pull the curtain back, share stories, provide information, and give people greater agency and control along the way to achieve the goals they have? As one example, we have started to execute an ambassador program with college and graduate students. We need to offer localized conversations as a conduit for exposure, access, and inclusion.

What lies ahead for Stackwell?

We are continuing to develop our product as we bring on more mission-aligned investors. Long term, we are delivering a robo-investing product that will immediately meet the needs of Black investors. Our mission is to earn trust and pursue a platform business model. We look to become the preferred partner for end-end banking, wealth building and financial services needs in the community by providing a curated set of products that are transparent, honest, and fair.

RON'S TAKE

It may be difficult to fathom, but the racial wealth gap in the U.S. is worse today than it was prior to the Civil Right Movement of the 1960s. In fact, white Americans have on average 7.8 times the wealth of Black Americans.

The ripple effect of this wealth gap is manifold, including access to capital, affordable housing, quality education, adequate healthcare, and more. The tools and platforms that have been developed are in common use today are overlooking the needs of the Black community by not addressing the root causes of uncertainty around investing and personal wealth management. In creating a platform that simplifies the "how to" and speaks directly to the Black community, Stackwell aims to address a critical need.

Historical stock market returns over the past 30 years have averaged close to 11 percent annually (closer to 8 percent annually when adjusted for inflation). For the long-term buy and hold investor, the cost of "sitting out" of the market exacerbates this wealth creation disparity. By enabling more Black investors to put capital to work, Stackwell will help to solve this gap.

4

GENERAL EDUCATION AND TRAINING

For an industrialized society to be healthy and prosperous, its people must be capable of producing wealth. For this to happen, you need a well-educated population that has access to good jobs and the ability for its individual members to better themselves by working and building their personal wealth, even at modest levels. Barriers to education, full employment, and job success prevent people from reaching their full potential and stifle the earning power of not only individuals but entire communities. Such barriers can take many different forms.

Education is directly linked to future income and wealth building. The U.S. Bureau of Labor Statistics tracks level of education, average weekly income, and unemployment rate. The results are stark:

Educational attainment	Median weekly earnings	Unemployment rate (%)
Doctoral degree	$1,909	1.5
Professional degree	$1,924	1.8
Master's degree	$1,574	2.6
Bachelor's degree	$1,334	3.5
Associate degree	$963	4.6
Some college, no degree	$899	5.5
High school diploma	$809	6.2

Educational attainment	Median weekly earnings	Unemployment rate (%)
Less than a high school diploma	$626	8.3

The very worst category is no high school diploma—the lowest income and highest unemployment rate.[17]

In order for kids to receive an education, they need to be in school. Education can only fulfill its promise as the great equalizer, reducing differences in privilege and background, when students are in school every day and receive the support they need.

Unfortunately, many students experience significant adversity in their lives, including poverty, difficult family circumstances, community violence, and health challenges, which make it challenging to attend school and acquire life-building skills. This can lead to chronic absenteeism and children falling behind. For decades, this crisis in our nation's public elementary and secondary schools was not fully documented. As noted by the U.S. Department of Education under the Every Student Succeeds Act, many states are finally compiling and reporting chronic absenteeism data. This evidence supports efforts to reduce chronic absenteeism so that all students have a better chance of reaching their full potential.

In 2015–2016, compared to their white peers, American Indian and Pacific Islander students were over 50 percent more likely to lose three weeks of school or more, Black students 40 percent more likely, and Hispanic students 17 percent more likely. Absenteeism increases with age as well. More than 20 percent of students in high school are chronically absent, compared with the middle school the rate of 14 percent and lower for elementary school students.[18]

Barriers to school attendance include family dysfunction, lack of safe transportation to school, lack of nutrition (primarily breakfast), and feeling unsafe at school. Gang activity, bullying, drugs, alcohol, and weapons, especially among older children, drive down school attendance. A data review shows that having a stable attachment with a school is beneficial too; the longer students are enrolled in a school, the fewer issues they cause.

Language can be a barrier, too. In the U.S., understanding English is an essential skill in classrooms. For students whose first language is not English, their limited vocabulary and language skills may prevent them from actively participating in class, socializing with peers, and learning to their full potential. Globally, English is as close to a universal language as exists, and for many students, learning English as a second language opens many doors. That's why in this chapter we highlight EnglishHelper, a company committed to deploying innovative education technology that reaches millions of underserved and deserving learners across the globe. Here are several VC-backed companies that are addressing some of the myriad education challenges with innovative solutions.

ALLHERE

AllHere operates a chatbot software solution designed to reduce chronic absenteeism among students and assist parents in the enrollment process. The company's software uses conversational AI and machine learning to power a bot-driven text-messaging platform. This provides schools a way to give one-on-one support, enabling students and their families to get proactive help and find the answers they need when they need it.

Headquarters and year founded: Boston, 2016

Founder: Prior to launching AllHere, founder and CEO Joanna Smith-Griffin managed family engagement and school improvement initiatives, and she taught mathematics at public schools in Boston and Miami. With what she learned from her own absenteeism campaign, Smith formed AllHere to support the leaders in schools and school districts looking to improve learning outcomes for K–12 students. Joanna has been featured in *Forbes*, EdSurge, CBS News, and District Administration, providing expertise on boosting attendance, strengthening student engagement, and combining AI, proactive nudges, and rigorous research to improve student outcomes. Joanna received a bachelor's degree in liberal arts, cum laude, from the Harvard Extension School.

Funds raised and VC investors: $12.1 million from Alumni Ventures, Boston Impact Initiative, Gratitude Railroad, Harvard i-lab, Operator Collective,

Potencia Ventures, Rethink Capital Partners, SoftBank Opportunity Fund, Spero Ventures.

Q&A WITH THE FOUNDER

Where did the idea for AllHere originate?

The idea originated with my own experience as a sixth- and eighth-grade math teacher. I was overwhelmed with student absenteeism stacking up and was equally frustrated by the feeble and non-innovative communication tools that were being used and getting no results.

What's the key problem that AllHere intends to solve?

We look at attendance and engagement as a skill-building rather than a motivation problem. AllHere is trying to solve the gaps in attendance and engagement. We engage heavily with families through 24/7 support with guidance and coaching over text and we have a platform that allows schools and families to engage at scale. We break initial enrollment and retention into a series of micro steps that help families complete the process through proactive nudges and assistance at whatever moment it is needed. Our solutions resonate particularly well with large, urban public school districts.

What differentiates the product?

Our chatbot is powered by conversational AI. There is a unique chat for each and every family that handles school-related questions. It can also be proactive. We deal with attendance through personalized intervention with families and have a large impact on outcomes.

What are the company's key accomplishments to date?

AllHere has worked with three million students from nine thousand schools to date. Our tools have driven a 17 percent increase in attendance. We have reduced failure by 38 percent. Our platform has even helped improve student GPAs by one-third of a point.

What lies ahead for AllHere?

We are taking what we've built beyond attendance and enrollment. Our goal is to support K-12 families and students during every stage of their education journey, from enrollment to graduation.

Our long-term objective is to grow our reach and expand its impact throughout the U.S. We intend to eventually leverage our tools in areas that include student health and well-being, IT services, and very importantly, academics.

RON'S TAKE

Beyond the basic human needs of food, shelter, medicine, and a livable planet, is there anything more vital to the survival and advancement of our species than education? Addressing problems and inequities in the U.S. education system is a topic of volumes of books, research reports, and philosophical debate. However, there are certain basic or "low-hanging" problems that are solvable at scale with the right degree of attention and clever use of technology.

By being able to engage parents and families on topics ranging from attendance to wellness to academics, AllHere is positioned to champion the forging of tighter relationships between schools and student families. AllHere takes a focus on urban public school districts where issues such as student absenteeism are acute, but the desire for practical solutions is real.

Joanna and her team, through their conversational AI chat messaging platform, will be setting the course for tangible enhanced educational outcomes across a vast population, one student at a time.

Disclaimer: Alumni Ventures invested in the Series A round of AllHere in mid-2021.

HOPSKIPDRIVE

HopSkipDrive operates a web-based transportation booking platform designed to offer ride-sharing services for children and teens. The company's platform allows school districts (the primary focus) and parents to pre-schedule routes for students with trusted, vetted drivers to shuttle them between home and school or other activities. HSD's software gives schools a full view of their daily transportation operations while offering the control and flexibility which is lacking from a fleet of yellow buses.

Headquarters and year founded: Los Angeles, 2014

Founder: Joanna McFarland founded HopSkipDrive after witnessing first-hand the difficulty of securing safe and reliable transportation for her children whenever they needed it. Previously, Joanna was an executive with OneWest Bank, AT&T Interactive, Green Dot Corporation, and WeddingChannel.com, among other organizations. She serves on the board of LA-tech.org and the Marketplace Industry Association. Joanna graduated from the Wharton School at UPenn and holds an MBA from Stanford's Graduate School of Business.

Funds raised and VC investors: $110 million from 1776 Ventures, 1843 Capital, Alumni Ventures, BBG Ventures, Energy Impact Partners, FirstMark Capital, Gaingels, GingerBread Capital, Greycroft, Halogen Ventures, Keyframe Capital, Maveron, OVO Fund, Pritzker Group Venture Capital, Skyview Capital Ventures, State Farm Ventures, The Artemis Fund, Upfront Ventures, and Women's VC Fund.

Q&A WITH THE FOUNDER

Where did the idea for HopSkipDrive originate?

The idea really started from a conversation among moms at a birthday party. Every one of us had transportation problems. There was the mom who got a new job on the West Side and was freaked out about how she was going to get her kids home from school. There was the mom who had two kids who had dance and soccer at the same time. I was feeling very guilty telling my son that he couldn't do karate because I had to way of getting him there on Thursday at three o'clock. As a joke, I said, "We should all just put money in a hat and buy a van and hire stay-at-home moms in the neighborhood to drive our kids around." Everyone kind of laughed that off, but my co-founder just looked at me and said, "Yes! How do we do that?" That's how it started.

The three of us who started the business have eight kids between us. At the time, they went to five different schools and were in about twenty different after-school activities, and we were really struggling with this. We started meeting to map this out, and from the very beginning it was all about, "What would it take for me to put my kids in these cars? How do we design something that we feel is safe enough for our kids? Is this safe enough and good enough for our kids?"

What's the key problem that HopSkipDrive intends to solve?

HopSkipDrive got its start in student transportation by addressing special cases like kids in foster care, students with special needs, students experiencing homelessness, school-sponsored internships, vocational courses, mid-year moves and other situations where schools are mandated to offer transportation. From that wedge, schools began increasing usage dramatically into serving all student transportation needs and to solve bus driver shortages as HopSkipDrive is more cost effective anytime there are thirteen or fewer students on a bus.

Having survived Covid school closures and revenue going to nearly zero, HopSkipDrive is helping school districts to solve the significant bus driver shortage and districts needing to adapt their solutions. Our solution is cost effective, climate-friendly (school buses traditionally operate with less than 50 percent capacity utilization), and provides time savings in commuting for thousands of student riders.

While it's a smaller piece of our business, we also offer parents the ability to book personal rides for their youngsters. This solves a problem that is all too well-known to parents who are working or lack sufficient personal transportation due to financial or other reasons.

How are you most differentiated as a service?

Where HopSkipDrive is unique, compared to any other rideshare service like Uber or Lyft, is through the vastly more rigorous vetting process that drivers must go through to ensure the safety and security of kids, alongside providing peace of mind for parents and schools. Drivers undergo very strict selection criteria, and the company provides real-time monitoring of every single ride to make sure that nothing is amiss. To date, the company has never experienced a critical safety incident. Furthermore, our software platform provided to schools helps optimize transportation for students by determining where a HopSkipDrive ride is more efficient or cost effective than a school bus.

What are the company's key accomplishments to date?

HopSkipDrive currently contracts with over 400 school districts, covering over 13,000 schools in twenty markets and eleven states. Since hitting a near zero-revenue bottom during the peak of Covid, we have retained every single one of our school district partners, and we've grown by a factor of three just in the past year.

What lies ahead for HopSkipDrive?

With little in the way of alternatives to traditional school buses, HopSkipDrive will continue to expand into new markets all across the country. The need for school districts to find more suitable transport options for their students, while controlling costs and carbon emissions, is a nationwide issue. On top of that, we are continuing to develop best-in-class tools that allow school districts to monitor and optimize their transportation offering and we have many features in the works that will be hugely beneficial to the schools that use our RideIQ software program.

RON'S TAKE

HopSkipDrive is solving several relatable and acute problems for multiple constituents: kids, parents, school districts and school administrators, as well as providing income opportunities for a special class of caregivers, who might not otherwise choose to work in this field. As a parent myself, I have seen first-hand the challenges that parents go through in finding transportation without fail, in spite of a full workload and other personal responsibilities.

Moreover, schools must manage budgets, find enough drivers, curb carbon emissions, and solve for individual cases, all while they have traditionally lacked much flexibility in doing all of this at once. HopSkipDrive is at the forefront of a paradigm shift that empowers schools and parents with the ability to make the best decisions for their kids and their communities at large.

Disclaimer: Alumni Ventures invested in multiple rounds of HopSkipDrive financing between 2019 and 2022.

ENGLISHHELPER

EnglishHelper operates an e-learning platform designed to help people learn English. The company's platform helps users to read and comprehend English while offering curriculum-based content. Additionally, the platform offers a tool that analyzes users' writing and suggests corrections of spelling and grammar, sentence construction, phraseology, and word usage, enabling students to improve their English proficiency and develop their vocabulary skills.

Headquarters and year founded: Waltham, MA, and Gurgaon, India, 2008
Founder: Sanjay Gupta, co-founder and CEO, is a business leader with over 30 years of experience. His professional journey started in the early 1980s in the world of finance, working with major companies in India, including the Tata Group, Eicher-Mitsubishi, Pepsi, and Motorola.

In 1996, Sanjay joined American Express, holding several different leadership roles in New Delhi, New York, and Singapore. At American Express, Sanjay was responsible for leading, consolidating and restructuring the company's Global Financial Operations. He headed Customer Service Delivery for global markets outside the U.S. and was chairperson of the company in India.

Sanjay is committed to the need for education to achieve the democratic vision. He writes a blog column for a leading business daily in India, *The Economic Times*. In addition, Sanjay is engaged with the cause of children and youth as an active board member at Udayan Care and the School of Inspired Leadership.

Sanjay is also a teacher and coach. He is a guest faculty member at Duke University's Executive Education Program. Sanjay also coaches senior executives and business leaders with a special focus on developing personal excellence.

Sanjay is an advisor to Acumen India and India Leaders for Social Sector.

Funds raised and VC investors: $10 million from Innospark, Omidyar Network, and angels.

Q&A WITH THE FOUNDER

Where did the idea for EnglishHelper originate?

Having had an extensive professional career in corporate, I decided that I wanted to give back by creating an impact-first social enterprise. I felt a strong desire to help improve education, particularly for students who come from the lowest income backgrounds, as this is the only route out of poverty. So after more than a decade at Amex in global leadership roles, I decided to come back to India from Singapore to focus on this next chapter.

I met Venkat Srinivasan of Innospark, who founded EnglishHelper, and together, we set out to find the most effective ways of utilizing technology to help students learn. We started to formalize ideas around English language learning initially in India, but we wanted to create a platform that was not limited by boundaries that could be used from anywhere.

What's the key problem that EnglishHelper intends to solve?

We are initially focusing on India and other countries with large populations of children who do not receive adequate education. India, for example, is a country with a very young age demographic. There are 260 million kids in school, of which 70 percent attend public or "government" schools. Half of these kids who are in grade 5 can't read at a grade 2 level. This represents a mass of young humanity coming into the world who are not literate or well-educated.

We chose to focus first on English learning because it is a commonly studied and read language across the country. For historical and professional reasons, it is a language that everyone can use, but not everyone can handle. We focus on using technology to enhance reading comprehension in English and are now expanding into other languages. We will be purposeful as we serve low-income communities at a significant scale.

Back in 2015, we conducted 100,000 independently run tests in partnership with USAID, in which we demonstrated the efficacy and learning impact of our solution compared with other commonly used programs.

What's your business model?

We make money through a freemium model. Our app is often free to schools for a period before we sign contracts. We maintain a low-cost base to stay nimble. Most of our eighty people work on product, technology, and analytics. Last year made enough revenue to cover our costs.

With schools now reopening after Covid, government schools are expected to have more money to spend on improving their tools. We expect to go from three times to five times our revenue in 2022, while our costs will remain almost flat.

What are the company's key accomplishments to date?

Having been at this now for 10 years, we serve roughly 10 percent of the 1.2 million government schools across every region of India. By the end of 2022, we will be working with as many as 200,000 schools. This covers over 30 million students. Of these, we expect nearly 5 million students to be actively using our app, which was just launched during the pandemic. We can now reach students at home at a massive scale. We have 100,000 teacher downloads who use our dashboard. We connect the school, classroom, teacher, and student.

The keys to our success are:

- We integrate with the curriculum. We do not add new or more for teachers or students; we simply make students learn more effectively.

- Teachers play a pivotal role, both in class and as influencers for study at home.
- We close the learning loop. Class learning is supplemented by self-study at home, assisted by our platform, leading to enhanced outcomes.

What lies ahead for EnglishHelper?

We are expanding on several fronts. We will start offering complementary learning products. In addition to English, we are prototyping with Hindi. We will support India's focus on foundational literacy. We don't try to change the curriculum, however how our app trains itself to read school textbooks in order to augment the classroom lessons. We are adding new capabilities that will enable students to learn using any content as well as provide personalized guidance to each learner.

EnglishHelper is beginning to reach outside of India to Sri Lanka, where we are targeting implementation in all 10,000 schools of the country. We also have a small footprint in Africa, as well as in Central America and Mongolia.

We plan to move our English learning tools beyond reading comprehension and into understanding concepts. We will be further integrating functionality to bring learners and teachers closer. This will enhance the post-class at-home learning experience.

Our longer-term plans include adding languages beyond English, as well as science, history, and other disciplines. We see geographic expansion opportunities in Southeast Asia, Africa, and Latin America. We eventually want to bring our app to the Americas, including the United States.

RON'S TAKE

Foundational literacy is the most critical building block to education and successful lifelong learning. Without this, those struggling in poverty have very little chance of finding opportunities to break the economic chains and professional barriers holding them back.

With widespread adoption of phones, even in the poorest corners of the world, the opportunity exists to provide tools that will help children from falling so far behind that they may never catch up. EnglishHelper has made astonishing progress in getting into schools and in use with teachers and students in India as a supplement to the classroom experience. With continued aggressive growth and expansion into other subject matters as well as new markets, the impact that Sanjay and his team will have will be substantial and disruptive to the low expectations that fuel the vicious cycles of poverty and illiteracy.

BRIGHTSIDE

Brightside provides an employer-based financial care platform intended to drive meaningful ROI for employers by improving the financial health of working families.

Headquarters and year founded: Chandler, Arizona, 2017

Founder: Tom Spann, co-founder and CEO, is serial entrepreneur with a social mission, having previously founded and led the healthcare company Accolade from inception to IPO, over the course of nearly 13 years. Previously, he served as managing partner at Accenture, where he worked for more than 15 years, including a stint as president of the Accenture Foundation. Tom holds a bachelor's degree from the Wharton School at the University of Pennsylvania.

Funds raised and VC investors: $75 million from Alumni Ventures, Andreessen Horowitz, Clocktower Technology Ventures, Comcast Ventures, Financial Solutions Lab, Obvious Ventures, Trinity Ventures.

Q&A WITH THE FOUNDER

Where did the idea for Brightside originate?

I was previously CEO of Accolade, a healthcare navigation company for company employees. A colleague brought to my attention that something like Accolade was needed for poor financial health, which was costing people an average of $3,000–$4,000 per year. Many employee benefits are simply not helpful or relevant for people without savings. For example, contributing to a retirement savings account with employer matches is not very useful for people who are in debt or living paycheck to paycheck. Data shows that 44 percent of people skipped a doctor's visit last year because of a lack of funds. This results in more stressed-out workers, who are less productive and twice as likely to turn over. This costs both the employee and the employer. I felt that mental health and financial health go hand in hand, and I wanted to solve the financial part of that as my next mission.

What's the key problem that Brightside intends to solve?

We solve a major problem for both the employer and employee. For employers, it is about financial equity. This is a major Diversity Equity Inclusion (DEI) issue since Black people have 10 percent of the net worth of white people while women are 50 percent more likely than men to be in poor financial health. We are on a mission to improve financial health for working families by opening the front door to financial services as a company-sponsored employee benefit.

How are you most differentiated as a service?

We offer real humans at the front end who are financial assistants who can help employees by understanding their financial goals and barriers and help them navigate options to make better financial decisions. They help find the best financial products for their families by building a relationship of trust that is not based on any hidden incentives like financial product sales commissions. We start with little wins and go from there. Our platform of financial solutions and products are also linked to the paycheck. This reduces or eliminates the need for credit checks loans on, allows for low interest loans, and we can also offer savings plans that are linked to each paycheck.

On top of this, we provide an app that ties this all together by linking a person's credit report with credit goals and monitoring savings. This results not just in financial wellness but effectively both urgent and primary care for financial health. People often face unexpected hurdles like being in danger of losing an apartment or inability to afford a car repair. We take the opportunity to build a long-term relationship. We find solutions to questions and problems. For example, for one user, we discovered an $8,000 community benefit that was available to her that allowed her to pay her rent, and she didn't know about it. Use behavioral science to prepare users to start saving for the next emergency. We can help people negotiate a car repair price, find the right car insurance, and dig up community benefits that people often are not even aware of.

What are the company's key accomplishments to date?

We have grown to serve over 300,000 employees and families. Our Net Promoter Score (NPS) is over 90, demonstrating very high user satisfaction. We put an average of $120 into the pocket of our customers and help them realize true financial health improvement. We are the only company in the employer financial health market that measures population financial health by looking at debt reduction, credit availability and more for people who use Brightside versus those who don't. We have seen a 34 percent reduction of people with subprime credit scores relative to people who didn't use us and a 40 percent-plus reduction in employer turnover across all segments of our user base.

What lies ahead for Brightside?

We grew by 10 times in 2022 and aim to triple that again in 2023. We will be expanding the products on our platform, for example to help people save money in the auto purchasing process. We are also considering geographic expansion to serve customers globally.

RON'S TAKE

Poor financial health is often not a matter of lack of will but of availability of tools, resources, and education that enable one to make smart financial decisions. For employees, this means the ability to save money consistently and borrow at reasonable rates when needed. For employers, financial health translates to a happier workforce that is more productive and less prone to leaving their job. A number of companies are bringing innovations to market that will empower individuals and families to be liberated within the financial system. By developing relationships with its users, including at the human level, and without conflicts of interest, Brightside is one tool that employers will be served in bringing to their employees to generate net positive results for all.

Disclaimer: Alumni Ventures invested in the Series B round of Brightside in fall 2022.

5

JOB SKILLS AND OPPORTUNITIES

I n the previous chapter, we reviewed the important link between an individual's level of education and their annual income. In general, the lower a person's degree or diploma attainment, the lower their income will be.

That remains true, but there are ways to defy the odds and succeed without academic degrees. One way to do this is to get specific job training in an industry that doesn't care about your educational achievement level—if you've got a high school diploma or a GED, you may be qualified for job training.

We have vocational schools, giving students hands-on experience to prepare them for employment in a trade. In America, a system of vocational education emerged in the early 20th century. Factories and trade professions needed skilled employees, and to develop them, high schools began to offer vocational education programs. In 1917, the Smith-Hughes Act became the first law to authorize federal funding for vocational education programs in U.S. schools.

But there was always an element of discrimination: Our two-tier educational system tracked predominantly low-income students and students of color into career and technical classes, and middle-class white students into liberal arts and professional careers. Black and Hispanic students were steered towards cosmetology and auto repair, while white male students were encouraged to focus on science, technology, medicine, and engineering.

Then vocational education became known as career and technical education (CTE). Today, federal guidance of CTE is through the Carl D. Perkins

Vocational and Technical Education Act. This provides federal support for CTE programs in all fifty states, including support for integrated career pathways programs.

In March 2022, the U.S. Government Accountability Office (GAO) reviewed the CTE landscape and found many challenges:

- Dated perceptions of these careers limits efforts to expand CTE programs at the secondary and postsecondary levels. Often, parents and students forget that these programs can lead to high-wage jobs without a four-year degree. They often think of CTE as what it was when they were young—automotive, dental assistant, and cosmetology—rather than what it is now: advanced manufacturing, software design, and digital technology.
- Too many students "lack transportation to get to work sites, which can limit their participation in work-based learning opportunities."
- "A lack of data on long-term outcomes and information on effective strategies for CTE can make it difficult to identify proven strategies for implementing or replicating these programs."
- There are challenges with attracting industry workers to teach in classrooms, because they can earn more in the field than teaching.
- "Running CTE programs often requires expensive equipment for training."
- "Students with disabilities often require additional accommodation.[19]

Job prospects for graduates of many CTE programs match that of four-year colleges. Not only can graduates step into a secure, well-paid job, but they can also be certain they will graduate with much less debt than if they spent four years at college.

Here are some innovative companies on a mission to reform CTE and open the doors of opportunity to all.

APRENDE INSTITUTE

Aprende Institute offers an online education platform designed to provide vocational skills training principally in the U.S. Hispanic market as well as in Latin America. The company's platform offers a wide range of both live and recorded online training courses that assist their students in acquiring skills needed to start their own businesses or advance their vocational skills in areas of high demand, such as hospitality, beauty, and other skilled trades.

Headquarters and year founded: Miami, 2013

Founder: Martin Claure, founder and CEO, got his professional start as one of the first hires at wireless company Brightstar after earning a degree in manufacturing engineering from Boston University and an MBA from the Kellogg School of Management at Northwestern University. He then went on to scale and successfully sell his own fintech startup in Peru and develop a publicly traded cleantech ETF (LIT). From there, Martin founded and ran MC Capital, where he oversaw numerous startup launches, of which over 75 percent resulted in successful exits. Martin transitioned to a passive role at MC Capital in September 2019 when he joined Aprende Institute as full-time CEO.

Funds Raised and VC Investors: $27 million from 500 Startups, Alumni Ventures, Angel Ventures, ECMC Foundation, Endeavor Catalyst, MatterScale Ventures, Reach Capital, Salkantay Ventures, Univision Communications, Valor Capital Group.

Q&A WITH THE FOUNDER

Where did the idea for Aprende Institute originate?

Aprende started as an online cooking school focused on the market in Mexico. I was an investor in the effort, and what we discovered was instead of attracting hobbyists, we were attracting focused, hardworking people who wanted to expand their professional skills and increase their income potential. We expanded to nutrition, healthy eating, and other areas. We then acquired a company doing the same but for skilled trades and beauty. This worked well, and it lit up in the U.S. Hispanic market. We thought this could be the beginning of something big. Today we cover gastronomy, wellness, trades, beauty, and other verticals. We rebranded to Aprende, I transitioned from advisor to CEO, and we raised outside funds and started focusing on building an amazing team.

What's the key problem that Aprende intends to solve?

The real problem is around the U.S. Hispanic market. I don't see a lot of products or amazing companies being built to help this demographic move forward. For many of them, having to use tools in English results in a very poor user experience. We are working to empower the demographic of 60 million Hispanics in the U.S. toward social and economic advancement. Only about 25 percent of U.S. Hispanics are English-dominant, while 35 percent are Spanish-dominant, and the rest are bilingual. Most U.S. Hispanics prefer to learn in Spanish as they are direct immigrants from Latin America. They moved here to pursue the American dream, and they work hard to provide a better life for their families. Most end up in middle- or low-skill jobs. They don't speak the language, and they face discrimination.

That said, they are very entrepreneurial—they have skills for cooking, beauty, and many different trades. We are building a product experience that is designed for them from the ground up. We are focused on teaching soft skills, as well as business and marketing, personalized for each use case.

How are you most differentiated as a service?

What makes Aprende unique is that we're teaching these things in an innovative manner. There is not a lot of innovation in the skills areas that we teach. How we do it is also very innovative. We design our curricula and produce our own content with instructional design and learning teams. Experiences designed for our users are asynchronous, where they can go at their own pace, but we also offer live classes that allow people to meet and engage with others. We offer practical training to put skills into practice. Students always feel like they have someone accompanying them along the way. There is always an expert a text message away. We offer a robust value proposition that leverages people. Students want to feel like someone is on the other end. We are also very affordable at no more than $50 a month for a course.

What are the company's key accomplishments to date?

So far, over 100,000 students have gone through Aprende. A lot of technology businesses start in Latin America and want to go to the U.S., but it is unusual for this to actually happen in a big way. We are a U.S.-focused company, but almost 90 percent of our people are based in Latin America. Our content is made there but is largely sold and consumed here. We have also attracted big partners to help build something incredible such as Reach Capital, Univision, ECMC (impact investors), and many others.

What lies ahead for Aprende?

There is a lot of room to improve our curricula. We would love to build new schools for teaching about topics like electric vehicle maintenance. We want to be closer to industry trends to have the most impactful outcomes. Also, offering licensing is very important to many of our students. We teach practical skills but want to be more helpful with securing licensing. We want to be able to provide a one-stop shop. We wish to help secure licenses and ultimately find the best jobs or contractor work for our students.

We do feel like there's an opportunity to be the reference for learning in the Spanish language. Today it is very fragmented. We will continue to focus on people who want to keep learning marketable skills that aren't coding or covered by higher education. Our goal is to be the biggest and most impactful learning brand in Spanish.

RON'S TAKE

U.S. immigrant communities are known for their ingenuity, productivity, entrepreneurialism, and, yes, willingness to fill critical skills gaps in the American economy. The roughly 20 percent of Americans who make up the Hispanic population are no exception. It is an unfortunate truth that cutting-edge tools and resources have not been available to help this group advance on the economic ladder. It is rare for U.S.-based technology companies to commit early or exclusively to developing products for the vital yet overlooked U.S.-based Spanish speaker.

Aprende Institute is blazing the trail for others to follow and is taking a hands-on approach to deliver invaluable educational instruction in the practical business and technical skills that are desperately needed for society to meet its needs. With such a severe gap in skilled labor across so many sectors of the economy, the courses that Aprende offers will play a vital role in bringing higher incomes and personal fulfillment to its users while uplifting critical industry sectors for the benefit of all.

Disclaimer: Alumni Ventures invested in the Series A-2 round of Aprende Institute in the fall of 2021.

BLOOM INSTITUTE OF TECHNOLOGY (BLOOMTECH)

Bloom Institute of Technology (BloomTech), formerly Lambda School, provides computer science education and training services to help students learn to code and get placed in IT firms. The company's services are available through online classes that cost the user nothing until they are placed in a job. The courses gives students hands-on training and placement opportunities in reputable companies.

Headquarters and year founded: San Francisco, 2017

Founder: Austen Allred is a native of Springville, Utah, whose startup journey began in 2017 while participating in Y Combinator, a San Francisco-based seed accelerator. This experience became the foundation of BloomTech's rapid growth. Previously, Austen was the co-founder of the media platform GrassWire. He co-authored the growth-hacking textbook *Secret Sauce*, which became a bestseller and provided him the personal seed money to build BloomTech. Austen's disruptive ideas on the future of education, the labor market disconnect, and the opportunity to provide opportunity at scale have been featured in *Harvard Business Review*, *The Economist*, *WIRED*, *Fast Company*, *TechCrunch*, and *The New York Times*, among others.

Funds Raised and VC Investors: $120 million from Alpha Bridge Ventures, Bedrock, Bow Capital, Buffalo Ventures, Caffeinated Capital, Chapter One Ventures, Gelt Venture Capital, GGV Capital, GigaFund, GV, Hemisphere Ventures, Imagine K12, Liquid 2 Ventures, Mastry, Neo Innovation, Outbound Ventures, Pioneer Fund, Riverside Ventures, S2 Capital, Social Stars, Soma Capital, Sound Ventures, Tandem Capital, Tandem Expansion Fund, TSVC, VY Capital, Y Combinator, Zillionize.

Q&A WITH THE FOUNDER

Where did the idea for BloomTech originate?

I was living in a small town in Utah, dropped out of college, moved to Silicon Valley, and taught myself to code. People I knew back in Utah wanted to do the same to get into tech. My original idea was to build an online coding school by simply charging for courses. However, as I talked to prospective students, it became clear that not everyone had $10,000 to enroll in school. That makes a lot of sense, of course. A loan of $10,000 or $15,000 plus interest can be devastating for someone working a low-wage job. I thought then that we should offer that students could pay a little upfront and more later once they have a higher income. This then evolved into our current model of paying nothing upfront, and then the idea really blew up.

What's the key problem that BloomTech intends to solve?

We are built for any adult who is looking for a career change. Some of these people will be interested in programming and data science, and a subset of those will have the right level of intelligence and commitment to make it. Over our five years, we have tested a lot of different things to know or predict if someone will be the right fit. We also help with the job placement piece.

We are willing to take on the risk that the student will eventually be able to pay us based on a portion of their future income. For a student, this becomes an elegant experience. Within about 20 minutes, we can run enough tests to decide if a student is ready to be taught the material. We offer three tracks: full stack web development, back end (built in partnership with Amazon), and a data science track.

The student has a contract to pay us back only once they are earning sufficient income. It is an outcomes-based loan, which will be forgiven if the student is unable to find job and no payments are required until they have reached a certain income threshold.

How are you most differentiated as a service?

While we're not a cheap option, we see our students increasing their lifetime income by as much as $4 million. The scary question for a student contemplating studying computer programming and switching fields is, what if it doesn't work out and they don't get a job? This is what we solve for.

We have invested heavily in our product and R&D. It is almost entirely live content, but we will make it more flexible. Our aim is to be like Peloton on steroids, where students can pick a schedule that is fully interactive.

We are also building out employer relationships to help our students get hired. We do not place anyone at partner companies, however. We help them build a resume and provide career coaches to guide them along the way. We teach students to fish and make it easy to network and apply to jobs.

What are the company's key accomplishments to date?

Our students have been hired at forty Fortune 100 companies. We've had 3,000 hired software engineers across the U.S. from both startups and household names. We can now connect students through our partners or alumni.

What lies ahead for BloomTech?

Right now, everything is working. Our focus is to make it more accessible. We currently only have full-time students. The median age is thirty-one. Targeting only full-time students is difficult. We aim to broaden this to a wider market.

In the long run, we want to be seen as a place where people can raise their hand and figure out what they have to do to increase income, train, and get hired in a better career without taking on financial risk. A tuition refund guarantee is key for this.

We also need to decide when to go international. We have done pilots in Africa, India, and elsewhere and have built a product that will scale well. We want to train everyone everywhere.

RON'S TAKE

Few professions offer such a steep income step change as computer programming and data analysis. The demand from employers, without question, far exceeds supply. Yet the skills for an individual to enter the workforce in software development do not necessarily require a four or even two-year college degree. It requires a specific skill set that can be taught digitally to anyone in the world with the right mindset and aspirations at any rung of the economic ladder. BloomTech's model of de-risking the financial decision for a student to enter this field is a noble mission that will bear great fruit for students, employers, governments, and societies that yearn for technology gurus who can help push products and innovation forward.

VEROSKILLS

VeroSkills offers an education technology platform intended to teach people how to code. The company offers "coding bootcamp" style online content to both novice and experienced students at no cost to the user. At the same time, the company offers a channel for recruiters to engage and hire newly minted talent to help fill the vast need for software developers and other IT professionals.

HQ Location & Year Founded: Birmingham, Alabama, 2021
Founder: Daniel Walsh is an experienced startup founder with a demonstrated history of working in the computer software industry to grow companies through sales and marketing. He has been a leader in numerous prior entrepreneurial endeavors as a President, CEO and Chief Marketing Officer.
Funds Raised and VC Investors: $500,000 from Eagle Venture Fund

Where did the idea for VeroSkills originate?

I founded VeroSkills about a year ago after having been involved with startups over the past 15 years. In my last company, we offered a coding bootcamp that trained over 1000 engineers how to code and then we helped to place them in jobs. When Covid hit, we saw a huge increase in interest. However, I realized that only a small fraction of the people who wanted to learn to code and seek better, high paying jobs, could afford to pay for the education that would prepare them. A lot of people didn't have the time to enroll full-time in a class or couldn't pay the tuition to participate. I was struck by what a shame this was considering how there are millions of open technology jobs in the US and across the world. I started brainstorming ways to take down barriers to education by helping more people advance into a lucrative profession. My goal became finding a business model that would work well to support educational opportunity.

What is the key problem that VeroSkills intends to solve?

Our platform is built to deliver high-quality professional training in software development at no cost to the student. We do this by offering a subscription-based service to employers who may wish to hire our graduates. We target medium to large size organizations that have significant needs for training developers and IT professionals. The only requirement of our students, in lieu of tuition fees, is a willingness to engage with a limited number of targeted potential employers. On the recruitment side, we offer employers the opportunity to connect with newly trained software developers at a far lower cost than working with traditional recruiting agencies.

How are you most differentiated as a service?

By generating revenue entirely through recruiters, we are disrupting the education market in a significant way. Our platform provides not just on-demand education, but we partner up our students with experienced mentors who are able to help guide new developers as they embark on this promising new career. Our strong impact mission has also proven to be of great appeal to many of our students.

What are the company's key accomplishments to date?

We are proud of the high-quality content that we have built for training new software developer talent, as well as for upskilling and maintaining skills of folks who are already working as programmers. Thousands of existing and prospective software professionals have already signed on and started engaging with our learning and community-building platform.

What lies ahead in the product plans for VeroSkills?

Our big milestone ahead of us is the July 1st launch of our recruiting platform. We will have 50 companies already signed up that each have over 500 employees and then need to hire at least 25 new software developers each year. We are also ramping up our in-house course content production, to go from 15 courses now, to be able to create 15-30 new courses each month.

What are the long-term strategic growth objectives?

Our 10-year aspiration is to be teaching a million students a year how to code, as well as other technical skills, to advance people into the IT profession who might not otherwise have the means to get there.

RON'S TAKE

Making inroads against inequality will be nearly impossible without breaking down the many barriers that exist to quality education that leads to highly demanded, lucrative professions. Few people would doubt the pressing need that exists today and will likely remain for decades in software and information technology. Coding bootcamps have proven that individuals can obtain the skills that they need to get started in this field without having to attend a four-year college or greater. If we can reduce the time it takes for students to get these skills, we will have made significant inroads. If VeroSkills can demonstrate that it is also possible to deliver such training at no financial cost at all to its students, then countless more people will truly have the opportunity to advance in life, while organizations will simultaneously be able to fill more of their critical staffing needs.

JOBBLE

Jobble provides an on-demand workforce management platform designed to connect businesses with people looking for flexible work. The company's platform allows businesses to offer job opportunities, select candidates that match their needs, and monitor the performance of these workers using real-time, mobile technology.

Headquarters and year founded: Boston, 2014
Founder: Zack Smith founded Jobble in 2014, having previously been a sales and business development manager and a collegiate entrepreneur. Zack studied entrepreneurship at both Northeastern and Suffolk University.
Funds raised and VC investors: $12 million from AXA Venture Partners, Boston Syndicates, E-merge Half Court Ventures, Harlem Capital Partners, Social Starts, Vestigo Ventures, York IE.

Q&A WITH THE FOUNDER

Where did the idea for Jobble originate?

I used to play basketball while at college at Northeastern. I realized, however, that I wasn't going to play professionally, and I needed something else to do. I started working events as a brand ambassador, helping to set up events, etc. For this, I was paid $15 or $20 an hour. These kinds of events always need more people, and that got me thinking along with Corey Bober, my co-founder, and Kevin Suffredini, who leads web engineering. We got together and thought what could be a cool company was essentially a "student staffing agency" for adults. We looked at the concept and found that the old antiquated temporary staffing space is itching for innovation. There was a building movement toward the gig economy. We realized that we wanted to work on this problem. The company has since evolved from focusing on the event space to the hourly work gig economy. We work with minimally trained gig workers. We provide lots of support tools within our easy-to-use platform.

What's the key problem that Jobble intends to solve?

The key problem is providing work and financial opportunities to the under-represented workforce. We focus on minimally trained hourly workers. We help by providing them with a lot of different ways to make money, but we also help in saving money. They get a high level of support for now and in the future by offering valuable products that fintech can deliver.

How are you most differentiated as a service?

We have the largest network of gig workers in the country. We provide them with opportunities that actually have both long- and short-term commitments to suit different needs and preferences. We stay flexible rather as opposed to operating as an agency that only helps to find either temporary or full-time jobs. We provide ease of use, short time to hire, and real-time hiring mentality. This is different than historical ways of doing temporary job placement.

We are not stopping at jobs but bringing a suite of financial products to our users. Jobble is simplifying products that should be simplified. There are a ton of financial products that they can engage with today that they don't even realize. A key differentiator is we look at ourselves as the PEO (professional employer organization) for the gig worker. We support employers by administering benefits and payroll, mainly for W-2 workers, and we can also offer other fintech products, such as payments, insurance, and banking. Workers don't need to rely on one provider.

What are the company's key accomplishments to date?

The Jobble platform has served 6 million workers and over 2,000 businesses, and we placed people in more than 5 million gig jobs. We are seeing 100 percent annual growth.

What lies ahead for Jobble?

We will continue to support the gig economy. The best opportunities are in local markets. We provide financial support and products that they can use by uncovering more opportunities. We aim to be at the center of the gig economy with a full-service fintech platform for gig workers.

RON'S TAKE

The gig economy has exploded in the past decade to become integral to society across the globe. From delivery drives to warehouse workers to many other sectors with short-term hiring needs, the marketplace of gig work can provide flexible, increased hourly wages and many other benefits. However, it was never structured to provide the same level of services that a full-time W-2 worker can typically receive.

Jobble is becoming an essential bridge for the burgeoning gig economy between employers and those they seek to hire. Through the Jobble platform, both employer and worker can quickly seek out the right individual jobs for each side's needs, including competitive compensation. Add on top of that, the range of financial services that full-time company employees generally expect, and the gig worker will finally have the security and flexibility they seek.

SABBAR

Sabbar is a Saudi-based tech startup that offers an on-demand staffing platform, specializing in blue-collar jobs in the retail, hospitality, and entertainment industries in MENA. The company creates job opportunities by reaching out to businesses and publishing their peak-hours and seasonal staff needs in a mobile app that connects to thousands of workers looking for flexible and hourly work.

Headquarters and year founded: Riyadh, Saudi Arabia, 2019
Founder: Mohamed T. Ibrahim, co-founder and CEO, is an engineer turned technology entrepreneur. Prior to Sabbar, Mohamed co-founded Dopravo, an internationally awarded digital agency, in 2008 out of Saudi Arabia. He has led key initiatives related to digital transformation for National Address, Saudi Telecom Company, Ministry of Commerce,

General Entertainment Authority, Small Medium Enterprise Authority, and Ministry of Hajj & Umrah. Mohamed graduated with First Class Honors in Engineering and Mechatronics from Monash University. The other co-founders include Afnan Sherbeeni (Product and Growth) and Abdul Rahman Al-Mudaiheem (Business Development).

Funds raised and VC investors: $5.6 million from 500 Global, Derayah Ventures, Seedra Ventures, STV, VentureSouq, and others.

Q&A WITH THE FOUNDER

Where did the idea for Sabbar originate?

I have a background as a software engineer, entrepreneur, and venture capitalist. In my previous startup, my brother and I co-founded an agency to develop mission-critical apps for the Saudi government. We grew this to over 80 engineers. However, a few years ago, I had a hypothesis that led to the founding of Sabbar. Having since experimented and identified our product-market fit, we came up with a platform to help gig economy workers to secure timely and flexible work in our current markets of Saudi Arabia and Egypt.

What's the key problem that Sabbar intends to solve?

Our platform solves problems for both sides of the marketplace. For gig economy job seekers, we provide flexibility and weekly payments. For employers, we offer immediate access to workers to fit seasonal needs, which can be monthly, weekly, or even daily. In the Saudi market, we focus on the hospitality, retail, and entertainment sectors, while our Egypt market focus is more on warehousing and logistics.

How are you most differentiated as a service?

Sabbar is really focused on the Gen Z and Millennial workforce who value flexibility and not getting bored in their job rather than long-term job security. These are workers who may need extra cash while studying or an additional income to meet their ongoing needs. Or they are simply seeking employment options that fit their schedules, which may not match traditional 9-to-5 work environments. Our unique IP is in our matching engine, which so far has matched 140,000 shifts. We have mobile apps for workers, and, for employers, a web and mobile app.

What are the company's key accomplishments to date?

We have become the largest player in our space in the regions in which we operate. Over 30,000 people have been onboarded onto our platform, which includes mostly students and transient workers who are looking for supplementary income. We have worked with over 300 companies that have hired workers through Sabbar, with more than 700,000 total work hours placed. Employers are very happy with our platform because our workers have no-show rates lower than 2 percent, compared to a 10 percent industry average.

What lies ahead for Sabbar?

There are many plans in our pipeline. In the near term, we will be launching a full version of our platform by year-end. For instance, we are developing a mobile wallet that will ease and provide instant payments to our gig workers. We also plan to work with our employer partners in developing an invoice financing solution that will allow them to manage cash flow through business cycles better. From a geographic expansion perspective, we are looking at Pakistan as a new market that can be well served by our solution.

RON'S TAKE

Across the globe, more and more workers are opting for flexible work that fits their schedules. Lower wage earners have traditionally had little to no ability to control when and how they work and earn a living or supplemental income. The gig economy workforce is contributing to the democratization of work, and Sabbar is on the forefront in the Middle East and North Africa by empowering such workers to take control of their livelihoods. While long-term job security may still be the preferred avenue for older and more experienced workers, many others, including younger generations, prefer to make the most of seasonal and short-term employment opportunities. Sabbar is among a class of companies worldwide that will enable this.

INCLUDED

Included operates an employee engagement and people analytics platform designed to capture and assess DEI performance. The company's platform delivers discoverability, transparency, and engagement through conversational AI-driven experiences, enabling organizations to scale their diversity program and seamlessly connect and retain their workforce.

Headquarters and year founded: Seattle, 2020

Founder: Raghu Gollamudi, co-founder and CEO, created Included after seeing poorly implemented DEI programs at large corporations where he worked as an engineering leader. Having successfully launched two SaaS startups in the U.S., Raghu is on a mission to prove that DEI isn't a tax, PR issue, or feel-good checkbox but an opportunity to build more competitive businesses. Raghu holds a degree in electronics and telecommunications from India's Savitribai Phule Pune University.

Funds raised and VC investors: $5.4 million from Ascend Venture Capital, Alumni Ventures, Flying Fish Partners, SignalFire, Trilogy Equity Partners.

Q&A WITH THE FOUNDER

Where did the idea for Included originate?

I was working at Microsoft for ten years. While there, I was asked to be champion for DEI and equality, but I realized that the organization never had the intent to go beyond basic staff training on this critical topic. I could see that diverse, underrepresented employees didn't feel included from a development and cultural standpoint. The current approach was not working.

I sold my last company in June 2020, which coincided with the murder of George Floyd. I saw companies struggle with inclusion strategy and especially how to measure performance. CEOs had to make statements to show what they were doing to increase the representation of Black and brown men and women. At the executive level below the CEO, leaders struggled to figure out how to execute diversity goals. Post-George Floyd, it seemed like every Fortune 1000 company hired Chief Diversity Officers. These people are amazing, but they don't have the tools and data to succeed. We needed to come up with a data-driven approach to solve this.

What's the key problem that Included intends to solve?

Our goal is to help companies build and retain diverse teams that represent their customer base. We focus on the entire employee lifecycle, which includes recruiting, onboarding, retention, and promotions. We help Chief Diversity Officers and HR leaders set meaningful, achievable goals. DEI is now part of ESG and 10-K filings. Companies are now disclosing their representation goals just like they do revenue reporting and set goals in order to focus and prioritize. Once they set goals, however, different departments grow differently. We are able to look at past growth rates by department and come up with a strategy. For example, an engineering team may need to focus more on hiring while a sales team may need to focus on retention. We work with companies to set goals, develop a strategy, and build an implementation plan.

On the recruitment process side, we make sure the process is equitable. We look at whether pass rates, for instance, are comparable between men and women. We make sure every applicant has a seat. Every step in the interview process needs to be inclusive.

How are you most differentiated as a service?

Everyone else who is looking at DEI at companies is focused on training, but we are taking a different angle that looks at employee engagement more holistically. We get into the facts and evidence to increase the probability of a diverse hire. We are democratizing diverse hiring and retention by applying automation with human involvement where it can add real value.

What are the company's key accomplishments to date?

We have been in business for 1.5 years and have seven customers from very different industries. We have a proven platform and strategy that is applicable for any customer regardless of segment. We raised pre-seed funding of $1.9 million, followed by a seed round of $3.5 million. We have recently signed our first six-figure contract and have attained SOC 1 and SOC 2 compliance. I was honored to be awarded "Startup CEO of the Year" by Seattle GeekWire.

What lies ahead for Included?

We are currently working with HR and strategy consulting firms on our go-to-market channel strategy. We will continue to build a product that focuses on the employee, with an eye toward onboarding and promotions, in addition to recruiting.

RON'S TAKE

Events of recent years, culminating in the murder of George Floyd, have called C-suites across the country to the realization that they simply cannot sit still when it comes to building and cultivating diversity in their ranks. Attention must focus on underrepresented employees when it comes to hiring, onboarding, training, retention and advancement. Included is taking a fresh approach that is helping to broaden the view of what is possible based on data, insight, and evidence-based strategy. The client companies that they work with today represent the tip of the iceberg of the need and opportunity.

Disclaimer: Alumni Ventures invested in the Series Seed round of Included in spring 2022.

LANDIT

LandIt helps women and diverse groups succeed in the workplace through their personalized career pathing platform. Utilizing a "one size fits one" solution, LandIt ensures companies can attract, develop, and retain diverse high-potential talent.

Headquarters and year founded: New York, 2014

Founder: Lisa Skeete Tatum, founder and CEO, previously was a General Partner for over a decade with Cardinal Partners, a $350 million early-stage healthcare venture capital firm. Lisa also worked for Procter & Gamble and GE Capital, and she founded her own consulting practice.

Lisa serves on numerous high-growth, public, and nonprofit boards, including Cornell University Board of Trustees, the Harvard Business School Board of Dean's Advisors, The Lawrenceville School, McCarter Theater, Stryker Corporation, and the Union Square Hospitality Group. Lisa received her bachelor's in chemical engineering from Cornell University and her MBA from Harvard Business School.

Funds raised and VC investors: $26 million from Alumni Ventures, Connectivity Ventures Fund, Costanoa Ventures, Cue Ball, Female Founders Fund, GingerBread Capital, Infor Global Solutions, Morgan Stanley, Multicultural Innovation Lab, NEA, Pilot Mountain Ventures, SAP.iO, Sofia Fund, Uprising Ventures, Valo Ventures, Village Capital, Wavemaker Partners, WeWork, Workday Ventures, Xfund.

Q&A WITH THE FOUNDER

Where did the idea for LandIt originate?

Like most entrepreneurs, I got the idea for LandIt from a pain point that I personally experienced. I started my career as a chemical engineer working for P&G. I then went over to the business side and caught the bug of startups and venture capital. I wanted to get into VC but was told that I only had a real chance to break in if I first went to business school. So I followed this advice, got into VC, where I spent 12 years, and worked my way up to partner.

After a decade, I was at an inflection point where I wanted to move on but was not sure of what to do next. At this time, I served as president of the HBS Alumni Board. We held a conference to celebrate "50 Years of Women at HBS." Over 60 percent of the women who attended said they were at an inflection point but were also in the custom of telling people that "everything is fine."

I got to thinking more about how to unlock human potential and how to give everyone a seat at the table. Most organizations focus on intake of talent; however they have traditionally been less focused on what happens to their people as they develop and what can be done to help them thrive and progress. It is really about access and not capability. I felt strongly that organizations couldn't touch as many lives without the ability to do it in a truly personalized way. My idea was to enable organizations to invest in their talent more in a more equitable manner.

What's the key problem that LandIt intends to solve?

We help companies tap into their largest resource, which is their pool of talent. People are not thriving as the current system is broken. We focus on the pooling of diversity at early stages by giving people what they need. We help solve retention through providing development, mobility, and engagement, creating a win-win situation. LandIt helps individuals achieve their goals, while the organization wins by fully utilizing their talent.

How are you most differentiated as a service?

We have two key components to our platform:

Personalization. "One size fits one." We meet each person where they are at scale. All we need is an email to get started.

Talent multiplier. Coaching is an accelerator, and we offer other platform elements, such as developing a personal board of advisors, and developing an executive presence. We bring people together to produce accelerated results, which reduce disengagement and quiet quitting.

What are the company's key accomplishments to date?

We work with organizations ranging from Fortune 500s to high-growth companies and nonprofits, and the results are the same across the board. Retention, mobility, and performance are all improved. On average, we have demonstrated a 25–35 percent increase in mobility, a two-times increase in engagement, as well as a 40 percent increase in positive sentiment. We help across organizations from leaders to individual contributors. We have shown success with diverse talent across locations and have been used in over 30 countries. We meet people where they are.

What lies ahead for LandIt?

We are focused on scaling by working with amazing companies. There is a proliferation of need with what's going on across industries today. Our solution applies across organizations and will continue to scale, globalize, and deliver on what we've done with personalization and acceleration of the individual. We have product-market fit. We are now focused on touching as many lives as possible.

RON'S TAKE

Cultivating a diverse, thriving workforce can be a complex matter that does not happen without significant organizational attention and intent. Lisa Skeete Tatum and her team at LandIt are providing the tools employers can tap right into to address the root cause of employee dissatisfaction and lack of productivity. This comes from a lack of engagement and direct, personalized attention to development goals. As the labor market continues to remain tight even with a looming economic downturn, companies will have to find new ways of serving and empowering their organizations to remain competitive. LandIt is one scalable solution for doing so.

Disclaimer: Alumni Ventures invested in multiple rounds of LandIt in 2017 and 2019.

6

CHILDCARE ACCESS AND AFFORDABILITY

I n agrarian economies that flourished for thousands of years, the home, being a farm, was the center of wealth production for the family. Children were born and raised on the farm where their parents worked, often alongside members of the extended family and other members of the community. If a child too young to lend a hand needed care, her mother could take her to the fields or leave her with a trusted auntie or grandma.

The Industrial Revolution changed that. Beginning in the early 19th century, adults worked outside the home, in factories. This wasn't much of a problem because as soon as they were able, the children were put to work in factories and mines too. Especially in textile mills, children were often hired together with both parents and could be paid only a few dollars a week.

In the 20th century, this began to change. In 1938, Congress passed the Fair Labor Standards Act, prohibiting child labor. Children began to be seen as a special class of person, and there gradually emerged a recognition that parents—and especially mothers who were entering the workforce—needed government support for childcare.

In the 1960s and 1970s, direct federal support for childcare was limited to policies designed for low-income families. There were several methods of indirect support through tax incentives for employer-sponsored childcare and offsetting personal income tax through childcare costs.

In the 1980s, the Reagan administration shifted the balance of federal childcare funding, cutting support for low-income families while increasing benefits for middle- and high-income families. Voluntary and for-profit childcare became a booming industry, much of which was beyond the reach of low-income families.

As Sonya Michel, PhD, University of Maryland, noted, the American childcare system remains divided along class lines, and "compares poorly with other advanced industrial nations such as France, Sweden, and Denmark, which not only offer free or subsidized care to children over three but also provide paid maternity or parental leaves. Unlike the United States, these countries use childcare not as a lever in a harsh mandatory employment policy toward low-income mothers but as a means of helping parents of all classes reconcile the demands of work and family life."[20]

Into this yawning breach are stepping two childcare companies dedicated to serving working parents while providing robust investment opportunities. Why is disrupting childcare a venture-backable opportunity? According to Kinside investor and board member Alda Leu Dennis, a General Partner at VC firm Initialized Capital, it comes down to being a hard problem in an underserved market. From an investor standpoint, she also sees that the male-dominated venture investor world is often less empathetic to meaningful problems that apply disproportionately to women and families. Even aside from any impact lens, Dennis believes in businesses that are recession-proof and that help both consumers and enterprises to save money. This, combined with a relentless and passionate team of founders who get out and hustle, is what led her to back Kinside.

KINSIDE

Kinside operates a dual-sided childcare platform designed to connect working parents with current openings at daycares and preschools across the country.

Headquarters and year founded: Claremont, CA, 2018
Founder: Shadiah Sigala is a serial entrepreneur who previously co-founded HoneyBook, a "unicorn" SaaS tech company that powers over 50,000

freelancers in managing their businesses and clients. She was the first member of her Mexican-American family to attend college, receiving degrees from Harvard (Master's in Public Policy) and Pomona College (BA in Latin American Studies). Her studies on the gender pay gap and sexual harassment in the freelance economy have been published in *Fortune*, *Forbes*, and *Huffington Post*.

Funds raised and VC investors: $16 million from Able Partners, Alumni Ventures, Initialized Capital, Escondido Ventures, Haystack, January Ventures, K50 Ventures, Magnify Ventures, Maven Ventures, Precursor Ventures, Techstars, Wellington Access Ventures, Y Combinator.

Q&A WITH THE FOUNDER

Where did the idea for Kinside originate?

In my previous role as co-founder of late-stage tech company HoneyBook, I made it a priority to have a parent and family-friendly culture. As a young mom, I particularly saw the acute need that we have in this country for access to childcare. The U.S. is the only industrialized nation that does not guarantee childcare access to all. I thought that there had to be a better way of solving the issue for parents and employers while also offering a more seamless platform for childcare providers to serve their families.

What's the key problem that Kinside intends to solve?

We are making childcare more accessible and more affordable for countless families. Kinside helps parents to identify the most appropriate childcare provider for their kids based on individual preferences, proximity, price, and availability. We are also negotiating rates with providers to help bring down the cost. In addition, it was important to us to offer this service to employers as a benefit that demonstrates the value that they place in offering a parent and family-friendly workplace.

How are you most differentiated as a service?

Kinside has developed a vast nationwide network of childcare providers, both chain and independent. We give parents transparency for finding available care, and we give providers the chance to fill open slots in a timely manner. Our negotiated discounts in enrollment fees are unique to Kinside and help bring down the financial burden on parents. The Kinside platform also offers seamless backend integration, including payments and customer relationship management (CRM) integration.

What are the company's key accomplishments to date?

We are very excited to have signed up over 13,000 childcare providers that will be connected to thousands of employers across the country. Perhaps more importantly, we are helping employees to save between 20–30 percent of the cost, which is a really big deal considering the average annual spend on childcare is about $20,000 per child.

What lies ahead for Kinside?

We will be focused on converting as many employers as we can to paid customers by developing the right integration capabilities, such as scalable account management and nurturing a pipeline of employee-led referrals. We will keep deepening relationships with employers while improving our ability to match providers with families.

RON'S TAKE

As any working parent knows, the challenge of finding the best available childcare for infants and toddlers can be a stark wake-up call and a humbling experience. Add in the dimension of cost, which nearly always runs considerably higher than even state college tuition, and the financial burden can become almost unbearable.

As the government dithers on whether children younger than kindergarten age should be able to access free or inexpensive school or care (as provided in nearly every other developed country in the world), families in the U.S. are often left to fend for themselves. This problem will not be solved overnight, but forward-thinking companies like Kinside are positioned to make an important dent in not only the cost but access and information to determine which daycare is right for one's kids.

Disclaimer: Alumni Ventures invested in the Series Seed round of Kinside in early 2020.

MIRZA

Mirza is a fintech platform helping working parents and employers by providing family and financial planning resources. The company's tools integrate family financial planning and childcare funding. This aids corporate policies for parental leave, fertility options, and modern parenting advice for employees, ultimately giving working professionals the tools they need to achieve their financial goals.

Headquarters and year founded: London, 2020

Founders: Siran Cao and Mel Faxon are mission-driven entrepreneurs. Armed with a bachelor's in gender studies from Harvard and a master's in social business and entrepreneurship from the London School of Economics, Siran has been an operations leader at Uber before becoming a founder.

Mel is a second-time founder, a UVA grad who cut her chops in the startup world, driving revenue and growth across portfolio management, sales, and marketing roles before getting her MBA from London Business School. The duo are now focused on solving the massive challenge of childcare affordability.

Funds raised and VC investors: $1.7 million from 500 Startups, Chaos Ventures, Pink Salt Ventures, Portage Ventures.

Q&A WITH THE CO-FOUNDER, SIRAN CAO

Where did the idea for Mirza originate?

I'm a first-generation immigrant from China. My mother was forced to give up her career once we moved to the U.S. After my father left, I saw first-hand both the long-term financial impact on the family of trying to get by on limited income and the toll the trade-offs my mother made on her identity. I now see this issue as a caregiver myself and how common this experience is; Mel and I set out to eliminate that tradeoff between paid work and caregiving.

What's the key problem that Mirza intends to solve?

We are working to solve the link between affordable childcare and employee retention. We provide financial education and a platform for no-interest, forgivable childcare loans that employers can offer their employees. We design childcare subsidies that any employer can get behind by aligning the forgiveness with key goals for driving revenue.

We focus on front-line employees, which include many single moms like mine, who must schedule their workday around daycare and school pickups. For these employees and their employers, childcare is still a day-to-day disruption. I saw this at Uber. I wanted to promote some talented hourly employees to roles with greater responsibility, but we often ran into challenges with managing around family needs. At the same time, I saw how people took out loans to get better quality childcare and the deep sacrifices that working parents had to make for their kids.

How are you most differentiated as a service?

We work with employers to finance childcare for their employees at no interest and build terms and forgiveness around the employer's key goals. Not only do we provide financial wellness education with our platform, but we also change the underlying economics for the employee. We charge a small SaaS fee to the employer. The employer does the lending, and we provide the platform and a complementary set of tools for the employer and employee to use. It is a turnkey program that allows the company to operate this benefit at scale. We give each individual employee a plan for how to utilize funds that employers are willing to provide, with guidance on how to use this with tax-advantaged accounts. It is a single place to understand overall family finances, including how payment and vesting schedules work and other practical information.

What are the company's key accomplishments to date?

We have been testing with about 100 folks this year. Our "Version 1" will be getting implemented with a major retailer client starting next year. We are also piloting and in advanced discussions with organizations that range from a solar company to manufacturers to school systems.

What lies ahead for Mirza?

We will keep building a financial platform and informational resource. Our roadmap includes adding helpful government support. In the longer run, we will be able to start to move from just early-year childcare to also helping people with costs for after-school care, camps, elder care, and more. From a customer standpoint, we are talking to major manufacturers and many SMEs with operational, front-line employees.

Ron's Take

The cost of childcare, particularly full-day care, confounds parents across the socioeconomic spectrum. The first question is how our country got itself into this position in the first place, where kids can go to school during the day beginning at age five, but for the first five years of life, parents are left to their own devices to figure everything out. The U.S. stands out among developed countries in this regard. Early-stage companies like Mirza and Kinside are working hard to disrupt this vexing issue, and we will need more ground-breaking innovation in the space so long as the government, with its inaction, continues to fail working families in this regard.

a Senate Committee on Banking, Housing, and Urban Affairs hearing. They bought up properties, they raised rents, they cut services, they priced family home buyers, and they forced renters out of their homes."[22]

The lack of home ownership is particularly acute for Black families, who struggle to build generational wealth. Neighborhoods where most residents Black have been heavily targeted by investors. According to a *Washington Post* analysis of Redfin data, in 2021, 30 percent of home sales in majority Black neighborhoods were made to investors, compared with 12 percent in other zip codes.[23]

In the United States, homeownership is one of the key pathways to building wealth—and for 250 years, Black families have been systematically shut out and forced to rent. When you pay rent, your money disappears. When you own your home, your money stays in your home, and you can pass it down your children. It makes a difference: "the Federal Reserve reports that the average homeowner in 2016 had a household wealth of $231,400, compared the average renter having a household wealth of just $5,200."

When researching the 100 U.S. cities with the largest population of Black households, the Urban Institute found that every single one had a significant Black and white homeownership gap. "In Minneapolis, a city that faced widespread civil unrest following the murder of George Floyd, there is a homeownership gap of 50 percent between white and Black residents. Even in cities with larger Black populations and more economic opportunity, like Washington, D.C., and Los Angeles, a homeownership gap of 20–25 percent still exists."[24]

How about affordable housing? One persistent obstacle is NIMBY, or "Not in My Back Yard." In the housing world, it describes existing homeowners "who oppose new housing development near their homes—particularly denser or more affordable housing." Residents express fear of "increased crime, traffic congestion, strain on sewers, overcrowded schools, and lowered property values and 'quality of life.'"

But when developments are built, however, these fears rarely come to pass.[25] Several promising startups, profiled below, are working to address the dual housing crisis of access and affordability.

7

HOUSING AFFORDABILITY

The United States is the wealthiest nation on earth, yet we h[...] shortage of affordable housing, and particularly affordabl[...] families who want to stop renting and own their own home[...]

The problem fluctuates in severity with the housing market; i[...] the market was especially tight, and many first-time and low- to [...] come buyers were priced out. In addition, we faced the problem[...] buying houses and outcompeting families for affordable homes. [...] CoreLogic, a California-based data analytics firm, in 2021, 24 p[...] single-family homes were bought by investors, up from a high o[...] annually going back to 2012. In the process, they drove up both [...] and rents for suburban families.

The issue became especially acute across the Sun Belt, whe[...] outbid competing family buyers, guaranteeing Black and Hispanic[...] chance at starter homes. Some local officials in those states began [...] increased regulation of investor purchases, but many conservative[...] oppose such controls.[21]

Real estate investors can be large corporations, local companies,[...] speculators who rarely live in the properties they buy. Some intend[...] flip homes to new buyers, while others hold them as rental properti[...] means families can't buy them.

"One of the reasons housing prices have gotten so out of cont[...] corporate America sensed an opportunity," said U.S. Senator Sherr[...]

HOME LENDING PAL

Home Lending Pal operates a lending software designed to create AI mortgage advisors that predict the likelihood for mortgage approval along with hidden ownership costs during research. The platform, which targets individuals of low- and moderate-income, empowers consumers to make home-buying decisions, enabling clients to get affordable risk data that is usually only available to lenders.

Headquarters and year founded: Orlando, 2017

Founder: Bryan Young, co-founder and CEO, is a former *Bloomberg Businessweek* "Top 25 Under 25" Entrepreneur and E&Y Entrepreneur of the Year Finalist with four prior exits. He built his first 7-figure company at eighteen and his second one at twenty-three. He has led global digital strategies and tactical execution for the likes of the 2012 DNC and President Barack Obama, Microsoft, Panasonic, Xerox, Zillow, CenturyLink, and others.

Bryan has worked for organizations including Time Warner, Adobe Systems, and Skyscanner. Bryan studied entrepreneurship and marketing at North Carolina State University and Colorado State University Global; he also holds an executive leadership certificate from Cornell University. Bryan serves on the Black and Hispanic Community Development Advisory Board of Quontic Bank, a New York-based digital bank.

Funds raised and VC investors: $4.5 million from BlueWave Investment Partners, CUNA Mutual Discovery Fund, Deepwork Capital, IA Seed Ventures, StarterStudio, TMC Emerging Technology Fund.

Q&A WITH THE FOUNDER

Where did the idea for Home Lending Pal originate?

I had been working in the mortgage space and consulting companies like Zillow. I became more and more familiar with the problem of low- to moderate-income (LMI) families seeking credit and the inability to obtain mortgages from banks and other lenders. Meanwhile, with my background, having worked for many years in demand generation as well as having started multiple companies in the past, I felt that I had the opportunity to create a business that could make a real difference.

What's the key problem that Home Lending Pal intends to solve?

The homeownership gap today for people of color is worse than in the days of segregation. LMI communities, in general, and Black and brown people face structural barriers that are very difficult to overcome. Half of the U.S. population is in the category of LMI and will face great difficulties obtaining mortgages and becoming homeowners due to the credit scoring system that exists today. Quite a few people would be able to improve their credit profiles by factoring in rent payment history and by taking advantage of programs offered by Fannie Mae and Freddie Mac. Many consumers are qualified for a mortgage but simply do not believe they are.

This is where we can help. We draw on an individual's full profile that goes beyond their basic FICO score. We connect them to banking services with personal feedback, and we're able to help match would-be homeowners with the right lenders who are willing to look holistically at an applicant's profile.

How are you most differentiated as a service?

Our consumer platform allows the user to create a profile that helps to determine an appropriate down payment, as well as find credit programs, local initiatives for closing costs, qualified lenders, and more. Users can ask questions via voice or chat, and we provide a "digital twin" that better serves the LMI community throughout the lending process. Moreover, we work with previously declined applicants and help them to improve their credit and financial situation. We reward with cash toward closing earned from good financial habits through our two-sided marketplace with lenders.

We take aspects of offerings from companies like Lending Tree and NerdWallet and tailor them to the LMI community. Our marketplace is up and functioning, and we are developing licensing agreements with many lenders, including Rocket Mortgage and Wells Fargo. By democratizing data among the LMI community, we assist with down payment, affordability, and finding opportunity. Our platform includes a conversational mortgage assistant that utilizes AI. For lenders, we are a lead generation engine that taps into previously underserved buyers.

What are the company's key accomplishments to date?

I am proud to say that we have signed up dozens of lenders to our platform and are in the process of rolling out pilots to support affordable housing with the likes of Fannie, Freddie, Ginnie Mae, Wells Fargo, IBM, and the Department of Housing and Urban Development. On the borrower side, we received 20,000 applications in our first eight weeks. We were able to pre-approve 12 percent of these, compared to an industry average of 1–3 percent. A third of these applicants, who are disproportionately African American, have already successfully purchased a home.

What lies ahead for Home Lending Pal?

We will continue to roll out more lenders to provide greater possibilities and choices for prospective LMI homeowners. We are also looking at providing refinancing and other services to fill gaps in this market. The product will be best-in-class as we grow our team to develop more AI/ML tools, broaden our IP and regulatory protection, as well as scaling up on both ends of our marketplace of borrowers and lenders.

RON'S TAKE

Homeownership is one of the driving forces of economic independence. As more individuals build equity while establishing peace of mind for their families, people will be able to break down structural barriers. Families of low- and moderate-income have struggled for ages to attract loans that help them to crack this critical life milestone. There is movement, and the public will now recognize these barriers for what they are and do something about it.

Platforms such as Home Lending Pal are enabling lenders to take a wider view of home loan and mortgage eligibility while at the same time demonstrating to individuals that they may qualify for home ownership through some basic education and support. Increasing levels of home ownership is not just sound for the economy; it is life-affirming for those of modest income who are working hard to bring financial stability to their families.

UNITED DWELLING

United Dwelling offers real estate services intended to provide affordable housing. The company's services replace detached garages and old properties in disrepair with new construction small homes and (accessory dwelling units or "ADUs") and handle every aspect of the process, including permitting, construction, finding qualified tenants, managing and maintaining the property, enabling property owners to earn more from their underutilized land, and providing a solution to the housing crisis.

Headquarters and year founded: Los Angeles, 2018

Founder: Steven Dietz, founder and CEO of United Dwelling, previously was a founding partner at Upfront Ventures. He has served on the boards of thirty-one companies in the automotive, financial services, retail/consumer, and alternative energy industries. He is a graduate of the University of Colorado-Boulder and serves on the board of advisors of the USC Marshall School of Business.

Funds raised and VC investors: $35 million from Alpha Edison, Alumni Ventures, Lightspeed Venture Partners, Y Combinator.

Q&A WITH THE FOUNDER

Where did the idea for United Dwelling originate?

I was a venture capitalist for a long time and decided to do something new. I was investing in the automotive industry in areas like autonomous vehicles. In 2018, I organized a conference on the impact of autonomous vehicles on society. One of the presenters got sick, and I decided to fill in. The topic was what happens to 1.3 billion square feet of Los Angeles real estate that would not be needed for parking. During my research for the presentation, I learned about ADUs, which are second residency units on an individual parcel. I thought they might be a good idea but would have problems addressing the problem because it would be hard to build small homes in lower-income communities. Then I started to learn what the impediments are to building thousands of homes. I started seeing how to get rules changed to make it easier to build ADUs.

What's the key problem that United Dwelling intends to solve?

What we present is a solution for affordable housing that doesn't involve the use of government funds. This is one of the largest problems that local elected officials face. I communicate by speaking with politicians and laying out a straightforward path: here is the problem, here is the solution, here are all the people affected by it. How can we start to fix a terrible situation, and how will this impact that official's constituents?

How are you most differentiated as a service?

There are three parties that benefit from what we do:

The property owner needs to be excited by it. Adding supplementary housing with no incremental cost of management means returns are very high. It's an important component for our customer base to see the advantageous economics. Similarly, for homeowners, most of whom have been there for 15–20 years and are disproportionately close to retirement, they want to know how to make extra income and can monetize land by putting income-producing assets on it.

Tenants generally want to live in a community but can't afford to live there. They are oftentimes trying to avoid three-hour daily commutes. Now more people can live in the communities they serve. Our tenants work very hard and are merely seeking a better quality of life.

The last constituency are our builders and trade workers. Our processes are highly repetitive from a construction standpoint. Because it's a repeat function, these builders become quite capable at it. A significant number of the people who work with us come from backgrounds such as unemployed, homeless, and there are some who were previously incarcerated.

What are the company's key accomplishments to date?

We have built 51 ADUs as United Dwelling with 267 more contracted. We also have a sister company in the process of starting to build 800 more. Right now, everything is in Los Angeles. By keeping our work geographically proximate, we can keep costs down. The only constraint on our growth thus far is the need to execute a complex business.

What lies ahead for United Dwelling?

We have shifted focus significantly to work mainly with real estate developers. They are the easiest group to work with, and this has proven to be cost effective. If we can routinely build multiple units per parcel, this will result in a meaningful amount of new housing. We want to build housing faster with fewer parties involved. We can make a bigger impact building hundreds of units with a few well-funded developers than building a single unit with hundreds of individual homeowners.

When we started, we set out to solve the massive problem of housing affordability. I fully expect other developers to copy our model, and they should. We are set up to partner with them rather than compete. A lot of what we do benefits from scale. We want to be part of solving affordable housing on a national level by partnering with a lot of other folks. Other companies are out there doing ADUs for rich people. We are focused on how we can build and serve the middle 70 percent of homeowners.

RON'S TAKE

Solving the problem of homelessness and lack of affordable housing is fraught with challenges. It requires money, infrastructure, citizen engagement, and perhaps most of all, political will. A wholesale rethink of how to solve these problems is required to start making a scalable difference. United Dwelling is working to reshape the thinking by creating more available housing at a relatively low cost. Their model not only requires locals and elected officials to get on board from a zoning perspective, but it also takes the buy-in of residents. It requires a two-sided marketplace of buyers/renters and sellers/

landlords. It is a challenging puzzle to execute, but the early signs are there that this can be done.

United Dwelling has allies to help them move forward collaboratively in the Los Angeles area, where they have just started to scratch the surface. How they grow organically or partner with others across the country to implement this repeatable model will be an interesting test to see if ADUs will make an impactful difference at a large scale.

It is comforting that both primary landowners and real estate developers are getting on board as more parties interested in bringing these housing units to market will lead to greater acceptance and an understanding that practical and innovative solutions exist to such a daunting and enduring problem.

Disclaimer: Alumni Ventures invested in the Series B-1 round of United Dwelling in spring 2021.

OBLIGO

Obligo operates a financial platform increasing increase fairness, trust, accountability, and transparency between landlords and tenants. The platform helps qualified renters keep their cash deposit and only pay if their landlord has a claim. It provides secure and limited access to a bank account, enabling landlords to bill renters up to the deposit amount in case there is a claim, effectively replacing security deposits.

Headquarters and year founded: New York, 2018
Founders: Roey Dor and Omri Dor are co-founders and brothers. Roey (CEO) is a former Israeli fighter pilot and an entrepreneur and operator in the real estate sector. He graduated from the University of Haifa with a degree in economics. Omri (COO) is a software engineer who has worked at companies like Google and Facebook, as well as in cybersecurity for the Israel Defense Forces. Omri studied computer engineering and physics and graduated top of his class at Technion – Israel Institute of Technology.

Funds raised and VC investors: Over $50 million from 10D, 83North, Alumni Ventures, Digital Horizon, Entree Capital, HighSage Ventures, La Maison Partners, MUFG Innovation Partners, Rainfall.

Q&A WITH THE CO-FOUNDER, ROEY DOR

Where did the idea for Obligo originate?

Our original idea was a lot wider. Omri and I were discussing the apartment renting experience as a whole. We felt like it should be more like an Airbnb experience but realized we should initially focus on building trust between landlords and renters. Trust is the reason why someone would come and stay in a room rented through Airbnb. It is because a third party introduces trust into the relationship. Uber is another example, with the idea of getting into a stranger's car. Or buying a bike through eBay, for that matter. The issue is trust.

What's the key problem that Obligo intends to solve?

We help to solve the issue of trust between renters and landlords. The specific problem that we decided to focus on first was the burden of security deposits. Early on, we saw this problem as the source of our product-market fit. Renters don't like having thousands of dollars tied up, which many times they struggle to afford. Even landlords see keeping a deposit as a burden, as it is cash that they essentially "sit on" for a long stretch of time. Obligo's solution removes the need for both sides to have to deal with rental deposits. Our vision is to make the move-in and move-out processes as simple as a hotel check-in and -out.

How are you most differentiated as a service?

Rental deposit alternatives were not invented by Obligo. Existing solutions come primarily from insurance in the form of surety bonds. There are problems with these products. Landlords might not like handling insurance due to occasional scrutiny or the question of "will I get paid?" Secondly, there is an issue around accountability. Renters frequently misunderstand insurance and when they are or are not covered. Landlords want renters to take care of the apartment and pay for anything they break. The third reason why landlords take a deposit, in part, is to check the renter's liquidity. The fact that a renter can't afford to put down a deposit is not a good sign for the landlord.

For these reasons, we did not opt for an insurance model and instead took inspiration from the hospitality industry. There is the hotel example of pre-authorizing a card. When you check into a hotel, they swipe your card and provide a credit pre-authorization in lieu of a cash deposit. This solution is more aligned with the goal of security deposits. The hotel knows there won't be any scrutiny and that Visa will wire the funds immediately. The account-ability piece is very transparent, and having available credit gives comfort to landlords that tenants will be able to pay their rent.

Our product handles both move-in and move-out. At move-in, renters can choose to pay a traditional deposit electronically or connect their bank account and provide a pre-authorization without locking up any funds. The amount of the pre-authorization is equal to the size of the deposit for potential future use by the landlord. When a renter moves out, if there are no charges, we will release the hold. If there is a charge, we ask the renter first how they would like to pay, including the option of no-interest installment plans. We will resort to tapping the pre-authorization amount only if the renter takes no action within 14 days.

What are the company's key accomplishments to date?

Obligo currently has access to millions of units through partnerships with industry property management software, as well as leading property owners and managers across fifty states. Obligo is the obvious choice for sophisticated partners who wish to embed a deposit-free solution into the renter's move-in flow. Our goal is to provide a holistic flow for both residents and landlords.

What lies ahead for Obligo?

In terms of go-to-market, we will continue to partner with property manage-ment software giants to become the new standard for security deposits across the nation. We are also looking more holistically at move-in/move-out expe-riences, such as renter screening, open banking data, and general collections, basically trying to create better experiences for both renter and landlord.

RON'S TAKE

Innovation is all about the marriage of technology and problem-solving. The system of holding rental deposits has been widely understood and accepted for decades, in spite of this placing a burden on landlords and a financial penalty on renters. Many renters simply do not have the savings and liquidity to tie up hundreds or thousands of dollars on a deposit for months or years. The requirement is also a source of economic injustice.

The Obligo alternative system to deposits will free up the housing market to more renters and will be equally appreciated by the landlords who keep deposits not for profit but as an insurance system. Anything that brings down the cost and complication of merely seeking housing will be a benefit that all can appreciate.

Disclaimer: Alumni Ventures invested in the Series B round of Obligo in the fall of 2021.

8

FOOD AND WATER SECURITY

I n Maslow's Hierarchy of Needs, the very first needs, which form the base, are physiological. These biological components for human survival include air, food, water, clothing, hygiene, sleep, and shelter. If a person struggles to meet their physiological needs, they have little hope of reaching the higher levels of safety, belonging, esteem, and self-actualization.

It seems hard to believe that we could have shortages of nutritious food in the United States. It's not a problem of overall supply: American farmers produce almost 4,000 calories per day per person. This is about 700 more calories per day than were produced in the 1980s and twice the caloric need of the average person. Out of that, the average American eats about 2,750 calories a day.

Good nutrition is not just a matter of how many calories you eat per day because both junk foods and nutritious foods deliver calories. Fast foods, processed meats, bread products, packaged snacks, and sugary drinks are all high in calories and low in nutrition. Not coincidentally, these foods have long shelf lives and are stocked in convenience stores found on every corner of every low-income neighborhood.

The problem of nutritious food is an issue of distribution and equity. Some American communities are grossly oversupplied with food, while others are "food deserts." As *Newsweek* reported, in urban areas, the U.S. Department of Agriculture considers a food desert an area with no ready access to a store with fresh and nutritious food options within one mile. In rural America, a desert is defined as 10 miles or more from the nearest supermarket. It's estimated there are more than 23 million people, more than half of them low-income, living in food deserts.[26]

Make no mistake—in food deserts, there's no shortage of convenience stores and bodegas selling packaged junk food. What's missing are the chain supermarkets that stock fresh fruits and vegetables and wholesome meat, fish, and dairy products. This is not by accident. Major supermarkets have been known to avoid locating their stores in inner cities or low-income neighborhoods, in a practice known as "supermarket redlining." The reasons are perceived "urban obstacles," including lower demand, higher costs of urban retail space, labor issues, lower profit margins from perishable food items, and risk of thefts in inner cities. Some people more bluntly call it racism.

"'Food insecurity' describes a condition where people have limited access to sufficient, safe, and nutritious food to meet their daily needs for healthy living." While all residents living in a food desert experience food insecurity, the impact is disproportionately higher among vulnerable populations of lower socioeconomic status, ethnic minority status, old age, and existing negative health outcomes.[27]

The amount of food waste in America is also extremely high. According to Feeding America, each year, 108 billion pounds of food is wasted in the United States, equaling 130 billion meals and more than $408 billion in food. In fact, nearly 40 percent of all food in America is thrown away.[28] Imagine what could happen if we could throw away less and distribute what we have more equitably!

Fresh water is also a problem. In some areas across the globe, as the world's population increases, access to fresh water has become a crisis. Over 1 billion people lack clean water across the globe, and almost 3 billion experience water scarcity for at least thirty days in a given year. A lack of clean water is a problem for 2.4 billion people, exposing them to water-borne diseases, including cholera and typhoid fever. Two million people, mostly children, die each year from diarrheal diseases alone.[29]

These companies are addressing these serious concerns.

EATWELL

EatWell creates nutritious meal kits that can be prescribed to patients to alleviate food insecurity, prevent diabetes, and reduce healthcare costs. The company's kits enable patients to enjoy fresh, healthy, and tasty cooked meals at an affordable price that are quick and simple to prepare.

Headquarters and year founded: Boston, 2017

Founder: Daniel Wexler, co-founder and CEO, brings a strong background in healthcare to his role leading EatWell. Prior to its founding, he worked in product and innovation at Zakipoint Health. He was also a process improvement analyst with Dana-Farber Cancer Institute. Dan is a graduate of biology from Cornell University. He also holds an MBA in health management from St. George's University and a Master of Public Health (MPH) from the Harvard School of Public Health.

Funds raised and VC investors: Under $1 million from Keen Growth Capital and angel investors.

Q&A WITH THE FOUNDER

Where did the idea for EatWell originate?

The idea started to formulate in 2017 while I was studying for an MD/MBA and got to thinking more about healthcare and, specifically, preventative medicine. There are 1.5 million new cases of diabetes diagnosed in the U.S. each year, and $327 billion is spent on treatment. On top of this, 38 million Americans who experience food insecurity are at a 50 percent greater risk of developing diabetes due largely to unhealthy diets. I knew that there were so many prevalent diseases and conditions that could be prevented with the right care and food choices. Diabetes prevention saves $6,000 per patient per year. I felt that the problem had to be tackled starting in communities where these challenges were the greatest.

What's the key problem that EatWell intends to solve?

I did direct research in the Boston communities of Dorchester and Mattapan to understand the choices that lower-income individuals make when it comes to food and what they might not choose the healthiest options. What I identified as reasons included:

1. Healthy food is too expensive.
2. Not accessible and easily available in the community.
3. Don't have access to a car or public transportation.
4. No time to prepare fresh dinner.
5. Don't know how to prepare healthy meals.
6. Feel stagnant, always prepare the same food.

I decided that I wanted to come up with a solution to solve these problems. We wanted to make eating healthy meals a part of the routine for those who do not always have the ability or opportunity to do so. We started in Massachusetts, which provides incentives to insurers to cover the cost of preventative medicine, including food, for eligible populations. This translates to no cost at all for patients.

How are you most differentiated as a service?

EatWell's solution is a meal kit that is sent to homes with all the ingredients to prepare a meal within 30 minutes in just one pot. We consulted with hospital dieticians and have a Michelin-star chef to make sure the meals are healthy, delicious, and culturally competent. We believe that food is medicine, and we provide educational resources through videos as part of the meal preparation process to support skill-building. We help guide our consumers with recipes and tips for preparing healthy food. Our aim is to create long-term sustainable behavior change through medically tailored meals. Our studies have shown that this will reduce healthcare costs as well as improve outcomes for those who consume our meals.

What are the company's key accomplishments to date?

We have taken an evidence-based approach to understand if our business is truly having an impact. For instance, we ran a Phase 2 study that looked at the impact on sixty-five patients from seven health centers regarding:

- Achieving food security
- Closing barriers
- Making food affordable and accessible
- Diet and food habits
- Disease prevention

We were able to drive a 40 percent improvement in food security among patients and a 20 percent improvement in fruit and vegetable consumption. We were especially happy about fruit because we do not even offer fruit in our meal kits. This was simply a spillover effect of our patients reframing their diets and making healthier choices.

We have served more than 40,000 patients to date, all without cost on their end. Soon we will be able to serve the whole household and not just the individual member. Furthermore, we provide jobs and hire directly from the communities that we serve.

What lies ahead for EatWell?

EatWell currently delivers between 50–150 kits per week. However, this is just the beginning as we focus on collaborating with partners to collect data, demonstrate impact and develop the ability to scale nationally eventually. We will serve patients across Massachusetts by the end of the year, and we will add New York next year.

RON'S TAKE

Access to affordable healthy food is among the biggest and most persistent challenges for lower-income families. The result speaks for itself in the levels of diabetes, heart disease, and other diseases that can be prevented with proper diet and lifestyle. While still very early, EatWell shows remarkable promise from the controlled studies that it has conducted. If "food is medicine" and health insurers demonstrate a willingness to support healthy food shifts in communities where it is most needed, patients and their families will benefit alongside society at large. Social entrepreneurs like Daniel Wexler and the investors who back them will be doing a great service by enabling the shift to healthier living.

NILUS

Nilus operates a food tech company focused on eradicating food insecurity by streamlining inefficiencies in the supply chain. The company's services include creating a marketplace and logistical tools to manage offerings and distributing healthy food at discounted prices to low-income communities, enabling low-income groups to access healthy food markets at affordable prices.

Headquarters and year founded: Buenos Aires, 2017

Founder: Ady Beitler, co-founder and CEO, is a lawyer-turned-social entrepreneur. Prior to founding Nilus, he spent nearly nine years as a project manager with Inter-American Development Bank. While there, he supported the reconstruction efforts in Haiti following the devastating earthquake in 2010. A native of Uruguay, Ady holds a law degree from the University of Montevideo and a master's degree from Harvard Law School.

Funds raised and VC investors: $6 million from Angel Ventures, Globivest, GV, Kalei Ventures, Preface Ventures, Myelin VC, Newtopia VC, Parallel18, Plug & Play Tech Center, and angel investors like Manu Ginobili and Matias Woloski, among others.

Q&A WITH THE FOUNDER

Where did the idea for Nilus originate?

I have been committed to social justice and humanitarian work for a long time. I spent three years in Haiti helping people to rebuild after the 2010 earthquake. While there, at one point, I was sent across the island to Punta Cana in the Dominican Republic. I noticed that groceries there were much cheaper than in Port-au-Prince, where people are far poorer than in the Punta Cana resort area. Despite being situated on the same island, it was astonishing to see that the population with fewer financial means had to pay more for necessities than in wealthier areas. It sparked a thought in my head about how to overcome this market failure, and I turned my attention to food deserts, meaning areas that are underserved by large supermarkets that can keep prices down due to scale and logistical advantages.

What's the key problem that Nilus intends to solve?

Food insecurity affects over two billion people worldwide, whereby food deserts result in people having fewer food options and at a higher cost than in more developed parts of the world. This problem does not just impact developing countries. In the U.S., the gap in prices can be as high as 50 percent between food deserts and more affluent areas. Because of a lack of distribution and volume, small grocery vendors often buy supplies at stores such as Costco and then mark them up to earn a margin. I decided to build a company that would try to solve this problem through the power of community, high-volume grocery buying, and distribution. I wanted to create technology to make this viable and efficient, starting in Latin America. The concept of group purchases has already been established in China and has led to the creation of three "unicorn" companies that are taking on this challenge. I wanted to apply this to the slums of Mexico, Argentina, Brazil, and all of Latin America to see if we could help these communities.

How are you most differentiated as a service?

We go straight to where we can have the most impact through people and technology. We offer opportunities to community leaders who are largely stay-at-home moms looking for both supplemental income and the opportunity to make a difference within their communities. By accessing wholesale prices through volume and leveraging centralized distribution hubs, we can pass along savings of 25–30 percent to consumers on groceries and necessities. This also gives large brands such as Nestle the opportunity to reach deeper into markets that they can't always penetrate as well as they would like.

What are the company's key accomplishments to date?

We currently operate in Mexico City and Buenos Aires, where we serve 75,000 consumers, including direct customers and their families. We have 600 active community leaders and are currently generating around $3 million on an annual run rate basis. We operate both a direct-to-consumer business and "social gastronomy" customers, including cafeterias, restaurants, hospitals, and schools. The business is growing by more than 10 percent every month.

What lies ahead for Nilus?

We believe that we have just scratched the surface in our first two markets. We will continue to focus on improving our business model and distribution through streamlined operations and greater volume. We think this business can scale quickly across Mexico and we are looking toward our next country of Brazil, which has enormous potential. Furthermore, we plan to test in the U.S., which also has huge disparities in food distribution, starting with the Miami market.

RON'S TAKE

For those of us who are privileged enough to live in communities that have abundant supermarkets and grocery supply chains built, the issue of food deserts is largely off the radar. For the two billion-plus people in the world who do not have such a luxury, it is a part of daily life to deal with limited stock, variety and having to pay a significant premium to obtain basic necessities for life.

The concept of collective food buying to benefit these communities really was popularized in China. However, the scale of the problem transcends both industrialized as well as developing nations and communities. The consequence of not solving this is having large communities that are stuck in a vicious cycle of inequality. Pioneering social entrepreneurs like Ady Beitler and his team are showing that mighty challenges can have simple solutions, but require the will and operational capabilities, not to mention the financial backing, to tackle such issues.

OFFGRIDBOX

OffGridBox provides a compact and modular, offering clean water every day in remote areas. The company's unit utilizes an all-in-one system powered by solar energy to purify water and distribute energy, thereby enabling households, businesses, nonprofits, and local governments to promote a sustainable and healthy way of life.

Headquarters and year founded: Cambridge, MA, and Kigali, Rwanda, 2016
Founder: Jodie Wu, CEO, has over ten years of experience working in East Africa on renewable energy and last-mile distribution. Fluent in Swahili, Jodie is an MIT-trained mechanical engineer and a social entrepreneur who sold the first company she founded. She has been an Echoing Green Fellow, TEDGlobal Fellow, D-Lab Scale-Ups Fellow, and C3E International Award Winner.
Funds raised and VC investors: $2 million from EEP Africa, Greentown Labs, Ground Squirrel Ventures, Massachusetts Clean Energy Center, MassChallenge, MassVentures, Right Side Capital Management, Stichting DOEN, Techstars, Good Energies.

Q&A WITH THE FOUNDER

Where did the idea for OffGridBox originate?

Our co-founders, Davide Bonsignore and Emiliano Cecchini, have been in solar technology for over 20 years. The idea of OffGridBox was born when our founders were tasked with installing a solar system and a water purifying system for six kindergartens in rural South Africa. Installation would take at least three weeks due to vast distances, training labor force, and material availability, making it more difficult to finish the project. They knew there had to be a better solution, so they started to pre-assemble and containerize the equipment, thereby going from a 3-week project to a 3-hour solution, making it perfect for project deployments and disaster relief situations.

I got involved after having sold my prior company. I worked with the acquiring company for 2.5 years as VP of New Products & Services, then moved on as a freelance consultant where OffGridBox was one of my first clients. In my first field mission with OffGridBox, I led a project deploying twelve Boxes in ten villages in Tanzania and then was asked to join the team as a "late founder" and get the projects off the ground in Rwanda.

What's the key problem that OffGridBox intends to solve?

The main problem we address is around water. Two billion people lack access to safely managed drinking water. And 759 million people lack access to basic electricity. We bring a solution that offers clean energy, clean water, and connectivity. This allows us to bring information and provide "urban" public services to rural areas. We are now focusing more on water because the water crisis is getting bigger and bigger. People need water purification and treatment and, in some cases, even desalination.

Our solar-powered standard 2m x 2m x 2m OffGridBox provides energy and clean water for 400 households. We help provide infrastructure for village power and water, as well as powering energy for refugee camps.

Our European-certified technology is becoming more known, and we have deployed in fifteen different countries, mostly in Eastern Africa, such as Uganda, Zambia, Tanzania, Somalia, and Rwanda. We sell boxes to partner organizations, such as NGOs, and international organizations, like the United Nations, but we also work with local and district governments.

We are now branching out into expanding our product line, to include a miniaturized version of our standard Box. This product will be more affordable and therefore accessible to rural entrepreneurs, schools, and health posts.

How are you most differentiated as a service?

We are the only ones who do both water and energy services in one solution. We are a technology provider, plus on-the-ground experience with implementation. We provide a pre-assembled plug-and-play system, plus training, technical assistance, remote monitoring, and impact measuring. This way, we are able to support partners anywhere in the world.

What are the company's key accomplishments to date?

Each of our boxes serves 1,000 to 5,000 people. Over 40,000 people are served in Rwanda with twenty boxes at the community level, including at health centers. We've purified one million liters of water in Rwanda alone. In total, eighty-four boxes are currently deployed worldwide, of which about half are in Eastern Africa. We've partnered with international organizations like the United Nations Development Program (UNDP) and the United Nations High Commissioner for Refugees (UNHCR), with NGOs such as Oxfam and CEFA, and with companies such as Aquatech and Google.

What lies ahead for OffGridBox?

This year, we will be offering three products:

We will sell fifty of our original OffGridBox units in the next year.

Our OffGridBox Mini is 1/16th the size of the original container and brings water pumping and purification of the world's most turbid waters. This will be an important solution in many developing countries as we bring more affordable solutions to our clients. We will be bringing our first generation of 100 units to market this year.

We are testing a water module in Italy that allows for the purification of wastewater and seawater through reverse osmosis, and we are preparing ourselves for the water crises that lie ahead. This will be hugely valuable and allow us to tackle all types of common water sources.

We were founded with a mission to help fight climate change and its effects. Now we are looking at a broader scope that includes agroforestry, and we will help bring back life into rural areas. We want to be creators at the nexus of food, water, and energy. Nearly 700 million people could be displaced by intense water scarcity by the end of the decade. By 2040, roughly one in four children worldwide will live in extremely high-water stress areas. Our mission is to start putting a dent in this.

RON'S TAKE

The problems of rural poverty in developing countries and off-the-grid regions are at a scale that many of us can barely comprehend. We take access to energy and clean water for granted when billions of people must cope with these challenges daily. OffGridBox has developed a sustainable, practical, affordable, and effective solution for making a difference in the communities they serve.

Governments and NGOs must continue to invest in innovative solutions like OffGridBox and their new "Mini" container if they want to continue making real progress toward alleviating water security in an environmentally friendly and inexpensive way. Solutions like these are available and getting better every day. The will to implement them must come from those with the power and ability to make such change happen.

9

PUBLIC HEALTH

From the late 20th century until today, the world has seen more progress in medical technology than in the thousands of years preceding. The digital age has revolutionized healthcare and opened possibilities for healing that our ancestors could not have dreamed of. And throughout that century, the world saw the average life expectancy get longer while metrics such as maternal death and infant mortality declined.

But now we're facing new challenges. Obesity and a sharp increase in chronic "lifestyle" diseases such as diabetes, high blood pressure, and heart disease have stalled the trend toward longer life in industrialized nations. After rising slowly but steadily since the 1920s, between 2015 and 2020, life expectancy in the United States fell from 78.94 years to 78.81 years, with a big drop coming in 2015–2016, well before the Covid-19 pandemic.

Additionally, as the gap between the very rich and everyone else widened, many people have not benefitted from medical innovations and, in fact, are having trouble receiving basic care.

As Physicians for a National Health Program (PNHP) reported, most industrialized nations at least half of their physicians are generalists. Until World War II, the United States had such a base, but that number has declined to less than 30 percent over the last 60 years and continues to fall. More and more U.S. medical graduates are choosing the higher paying, more attractive lifestyles of other specialties instead of pursuing primary care as a specialty. We now have a specialist-dominated system without anywhere near the number of generalists needed.[30]

And who suffers most under such a system? Poor people who cannot afford to pay high premiums for "gold-level" health plans and may live miles from a primary care physician. For many patients across the country, easy healthcare access is not a reality. Patients living in rural areas—with higher levels of lifestyle diseases and opioid addictions—are disproportionately more likely to struggle to access their clinician than those living in urban or suburban areas. Lack of transportation can keep patients from seeing their doctors. Patients who face financial barriers, cannot drive, or otherwise cannot obtain transportation to the clinician's office often go without care.

As an investor who puts venture dollars to work solving public health crises, Dr. Joy Ippolito cares deeply about paying it forward and helping to create and support impact for individuals, families, and communities that are marginalized and misunderstood. "Too often, value judgments are placed upon them by outsiders as if poor outcomes are a result of personal decisions, rather than understanding the external forces that infringe and impinge upon their daily lives."

In her capacity as social impact investment director of the American Family Insurance Institute for Corporate and Social Impact, Dr. Ippolito met the founders of Vincere Health, Jake Keteyian and Shalen De Silva. They had just graduated from their MPH program at Harvard and were eager to start building their vision. "The company was largely still just an idea at that point, but I was struck by how fundamentally they understood the problem of behavioral health change for lower-income populations. They didn't offer judgment; they wanted to understand customers' lives and offer a responsive solution. They had given up lucrative careers in business and finance to help change the world. And they had a compelling plan for how to get there. Over three years later, they remain the epitome of what we look for in founders and startup companies—they and their team have the heart, smarts, and determination for creating a successful business that champions social impact and financial return equally."

Here's more about a select group of companies, including Vincere Health, working to address critical gaps in the healthcare delivery system.

NURSE-1-1

"Nurse-1-1 is a conversational marketing company for healthcare that is bringing nurses to the frontlines of digital health. Through a nationwide network of nurses and a HIPAA-compliant complete customer service platform, Nurse-1-1 offers a live nurse chat tool that can be embedded directly into other digital platforms, which helps patients make better decisions leading to increased adherence. At-home testing, pharmaceutical, and digital health companies of all sizes rely on Nurse-1-1 to improve education, increase adherence, and increase patient satisfaction."[31]

Headquarters and year founded: Boston, 2016

Founder: Michael Sheeley has a mission to connect health-concerned consumers to nurses in their own communities based on personal experience he and his wife had when their daughter was born with a congenital heart defect. "Texting with our friend Kim, who happened to be a pediatric nurse practitioner, helped us get through the scary and confusing healthcare system. I want everyone to have access to these same caring and compassionate professionals in our communities."

Michael previously co-founded two venture-backed companies as co-founder and head of product at the health and fitness-tracking platform RunKeeper and co-founder and CEO of the AI-powered local restaurant ordering platform Chef Nightly. Michael also served as head of product at the venture-backed startup Mobee, a retail app that rewards consumers by providing feedback to local retailers.

Funds raised and VC investors: A total of $3.5 million has been raised, including a seed round led by Argon Ventures, Hyperplane Venture Capital, and York IE.

Q&A WITH THE FOUNDER

Where did the idea for Nurse-1-1 originate?

The idea for Nurse-1-1 dates back to the birth of my daughter, Lydia, who was born with a congenital heart defect and required heart surgery at just three months old. The healthcare system at the time was complicated and lacked empathy, and I needed more than just clinical results to get me through.

Thankfully I had my friend Kim, a pediatric nurse practitioner, who was there to help support my family every step of the way. Kim, who eventually became my co-founder, opened my eyes to the need for empathy and access in healthcare, and thus Nurse-1-1 was born.

What's the key problem that Nurse-1-1 intends to solve?

Non-adherence to medications costs the healthcare system $300 billion annually. While digital healthcare and online pharma are great initial options, they come with drawbacks. Add Covid-19 to the mix, and it is near impossible to get your health questions answered unless you are sitting right next to a doctor or a nurse.

Nurse-1-1 is changing that dynamic. We are providing access to care exactly when patients need it. Patients need the empathy and expertise of a nurse to help answer their questions about side effects, affordability, and more. Nurse-1-1 is marrying the benefits of at-home care with the influence of professional opinions.

We drive patient activation and adherence. Our nurse network educates patients, helping our partner companies guide their patients through their digital health journey—for example, increasing filled prescriptions, successfully returning an at-home test to the lab, or navigating patients to higher-value services. We provide our customers with unprecedented access to our nationwide nursing network by bringing conversational marketing to healthcare.

How are you most differentiated as a service?

On the product side, patients get to connect with an actual nurse—not just a call center employee with a checklist or an AI bot. Human-to-human interaction with trust, empathy, and influence. We are HIPAA-compliant and have technical expertise focused on supporting and caring for patients that other conversational marketing companies don't have. We also bring data-driven analytics that help companies market better.

Our team has a background in consumer tech (Uber, RunKeeper), so building tech people actually want, which is different than clinical solutions. One of our co-founders is a nurse, and our company has a nationwide network of nurses that helps ensure the patient is front and center in every decision the company makes

What are the company's key accomplishments to date?

In 2021, our platform conducted over 10,000 patient consultations through our partnerships with digital health, at-home testing, and pharma companies. On average, patients were connected with a nurse in fewer than eight seconds. Our network of nurses is strong and growing at almost 3,000 nationwide.

In a program where we aimed to divert patients away from the ER when it wasn't appropriate, 95 percent of those patients chose other, more appropriate forms of care (e.g., a telemedicine visit with a provider) when they initially thought they needed to go to the ER.

Finally, Nurse-1-1 enjoys a Net Promoter Score of 58, meaning "excellent," emphasizing how much patients enjoy the experience and are likely to refer a friend. A controlled study by one of Nurse-1-1's largest digital health partners showed a 255 percent increase in sign-ups. Both factors highlight Nurse-1-1's ability to strongly engage with and influence patients.

What lies ahead for Nurse-1-1?

In the future, we envision Nurse-1-1 as a core element to all patient touchpoints within digital healthcare. Our goal is to build a product that allows the nurse to walk any patient through any digital health experience. We aim to be the partner of choice for digital health companies to build a full-service customer service platform that better serves their patients.

As our live chat tool is embedded on more and more major health platforms, over time, this will allow for a nurse to chat with a patient as they travel from health service to health service. This is similar to the way a nurse would walk a patient from radiology to the operating room and back to their room to rest. We'll do the same for patients using digital health services, pairing patients across the globe with a trusted nurse, just like I had with Kim. This type of access to nurses shouldn't just be for people privileged enough to live in neighborhoods with world-class providers. Everyone should have this type of access.

For each of the past 20 years, the Gallup poll has rated nursing as the most trusted profession in America. We are bringing this trust into the growing digital health market, pioneering a new category in healthcare with our patient-centric and dialogue-driven approach to care. In the future, we envision Nurse-1-1 as a core element to all patient touchpoints within digital healthcare.

RON'S TAKE

As nearly anyone who has sought any medical diagnosis or treatment can attest, nurses are vital in not only providing essential care but in communicating accurate, timely information with patience and empathy. The shift into digital health has been critical for many in the population for numerous reasons. It is precisely the ability to access professional support remotely, especially when face-to-face visits are not essential, that allows people to speak with their providers. For lower-income individuals, this solves issues of transportation, time out of work, and uncertain insurance coverage. For Nurse-1-1, patient adherence to medication is at the forefront and is a costly problem that must be solved to save lives and improve health outcomes. A team of prepared, round-the-clock nurses who can support health communication and delivery will become integral, while Nurse-1-1 also provides nurses the opportunity to enhance their income within the confines of their own homes and schedule availabilities.

Disclaimer: I invested with personal funds in the Series Seed round of Nurse-1-1 in early 2022.

HEALTH IN HER HUE

Health in Her HUE operates an online platform that helps Black women access healthcare providers, telehealth services, and health content, enabling members to connect and communicate with community doctors comfortably.

Headquarters and year founded: New York, 2018

Founder: Ashlee Wisdom is a public health innovator who is committed to dismantling racist systems. She is committed to building equitable solutions to overcome anti-Black racism and injustice in healthcare, with a goal of a more equitable and just healthcare ecosystem, guaranteeing everyone can care they need and deserve. In addition to working in public health research and policy at several leading institutions, she is currently a fellow with the Aspen Institute. Ashlee graduated from Howard University and holds a master's degree in healthcare policy & management from NYU.

Funds Raised and VC Investors: Over $1 million from BLXVC, Genius Guild, Graham & Walker Venture Fund, Pipeline Angels, Seae Ventures, Unseen Capital.

Q&A WITH THE FOUNDER

Where did the idea for Health in Her HUE originate?

I have a background in public health and have worked in healthcare my entire career. This idea came while I was in grad school at NYU and working in a particular department at an academic medical center that was notorious for not being the friendliest to women of color faculty members and employees. They had a revolving door for Black employees. I had to work there in order to satisfy internship requirements for my master's degree. During this time, I broke out in hives and went to see an allergist. I was told that I wasn't allergic to anything and to go home and take two Allegras. However, after I left that job, the hives stopped. It turned out that it was tension and stress from my job where I was encountering regular subtle racism that was creating problems for my health.

As a grad student, I was reading scientific papers about disparate outcomes for Black women and women of color. On top of that, I was on the email list for New York alumni of Howard University, where I attended college. About twice a week, people would ask for referrals to Black doctors or therapists. It got me wondering why we have to rely on social networks in order to find trusted providers. This got the wheels turning, hyper-aware of Black women who are not getting adequate care. I began to wonder what I can do to take information from the "ivory tower" and make the highest quality health content and healthcare for Black women more accessible.

What's the key problem that Health in Her HUE intends to solve?

Our platform is based on the creation of content from the lived experience of a Black woman. We talk about the four C's: Connections, Content, Community, and Consults. The product offers content (evidence-based health content tailored to women of color). We help our users find culturally sensitive providers by specialty, location, and accepted insurance. We offer a community forum for those with similar experiences or diagnoses to connect and not feel isolated. It is shocking that 25 percent of Black Americans live in areas with a shortage of primary care providers, let alone many critical specialist providers. Our platform is meant to help fill this gap.

How are you most differentiated as a service?

We started with content and becoming the trusted source for health information navigation for women of color. We then built a community around HIHH to better understand the collective pain points from Black women. We then learned from our community, who struggled to find providers who "look like me." Our provider directory helps our users to find a Black doctor or therapist, and we offer a safe space through our community forum.

We offer a "freemium" model thanks to our new premium web subscription. Free users have access to our directory, community forums, and three pieces of content per month. Paid users have unlimited access, including written content, videos, and our event series. Once we raise our full seed round, we will begin to offer a telehealth experience. Our virtual care squad program combines evidence-based health information with guided peer support for women who are on a similar journey based on their condition. The women get access to curricula designed by a board-certified physician who provides them with a squad of peers and a HIHH facilitator who will guide them through the content and live discussions. We are currently running internal pilots with this and have our first health plan pilot to begin scaling this offering.

What are the company's key accomplishments to date?

We are a very scrappy team, and when we released our first MVP, the platform suddenly went viral. We had six doctors who posted on Instagram and Twitter, and within two weeks, we had registered 34,000 logins with email addresses. We had 55,000 people log in to try the first product. It was a disjointed experience, so we created a downloadable app last year, which launched in May 2021. Today we have 1,000 providers and thousands more users. Our latest version just launched this past April.

What lies ahead for Health in Her HUE?

We are purely D2C right now, but we are making headways in our enterprise strategy. We plan to sell to employers and health plans and have secured our first health plan pilot. We are looking forward to piloting telehealth as well.

RON'S TAKE

Few aspects of healthcare delivery can be as frustrating as not getting the personalized attention and care one expects and deserves, regardless of race, gender, nationality, or income. Finding a provider who is culturally sensitive to the concerns of women of color, particularly, is one of the most difficult challenges for many patients. In fact, Black patients are proven to have better outcomes when treated by Black doctors. As one example, infant mortality rates have been shown to be reduced by as much as 50 percent when Black obstetricians are working with Black patients. While bias takes many forms, the lack of culturally sensitive care can simply come down to a lack of shared experience and identity. Health in Her HUE is unapologetically tackling this problem head-on. As a resource for finding providers, as well as information and community around health topics, the company is embarking on becoming the leader in redefining the structural difficulties of those who are overlooked in obtaining the right level of care and support at the time when they need it.

VINCERE HEALTH

Vincere Health is pioneering behavior change incentivization to help people reclaim a smoke-free and vape-free lifestyle. The Vincere Health EARN program is a tech-enabled behavioral health platform that bundles a carbon (CO) monitoring breath pen, health coaching, and financial incentives to improve outcomes for smoking cessation or reduction.

Headquarters and year founded: Boston, 2019
Founders: Shalen De Silva, CEO, and Jacob Keteyian, president.

Shalen is a recovering banker who worked in M&A and Leveraged Finance at Deloitte, BNP, and SMBC. He co-founded Global Clinic so he could deliver free cataract and cleft surgeries as well as primary eye and dental care around remote parts of Asia. His work with Global Clinic inspired him to leave the world of banking and focus his career to healthcare. Shalen holds math, finance, and public health degrees from LSE, Cambridge, and Harvard.

Jake worked as a consultant in healthcare strategy and technology before obtaining his master's degree at Harvard. He prioritized innovative care delivery models and early value-based care initiatives for payers, providers, and state agencies. He values building teams and tech that enable remote care options for vulnerable populations.

Funds raised and VC investors: $4.3 million from Alchemist Accelerator, Alumni Ventures, Am Fam Institute, Celtic House Asia Partners, Flare Capital Partners, Harvard i-Lab, HBS Alumni Angels, Purpose Built Ventures, SixThirty Ventures, Techstars, Victress Capital.

Q&A WITH THE CO-FOUNDER, SHALEN DE SILVA

Where did the idea for Vincere Health originate?

Jake Keteyian and I arrived at it from different places. I had been a banker and had also worked in global health in several emerging markets. I saw serious needs in countries where people had no access to basic medical care and expertise. Through this lens, I had always envisioned a system that empowers people with better choices. Financial incentives were an interesting way to nudge people into certain directions. I wanted to use instant rewards, health monitoring, and behavioral sciences principles to encourage people to lead healthier lifestyles.

Coming at this from working in U.S. healthcare strategy and Medicaid policy and payment innovation, Jake recognized that digital health was not directed at certain vulnerable groups. Together, we saw the opportunity to apply both technology and academic research to a low-income population that was trapped in a void of health innovation.

What's the key problem that Vincere intends to solve?

Our most important observation since we began this endeavor is that human connection is the most important thing when working with patients to change behavior. The patient needs a qualified health professional to engage with them directly, which is hard to substitute with technology. Everything we are doing is to maximize opportunities for a human relationship. We are building digital experiences and behavioral nudges that enable and increase the likelihood that a patient can have a relationship with a clinician. This includes the population that normally can't afford this. Remote monitoring helps track outcomes and drives efficiency and transparency. Vincere provides extrinsic motivation for the patient to engage, learn and discover their own intrinsic motivation.

How are you most differentiated as a service?

We have set ourselves apart by being able to find government and insurance industry sponsors who see the highest financial pain from a population of their constituents and members who remain unhealthy. We have worked with state agencies, including Medicaid, and have earned their trust to prove that we can move the needle on outcomes for a low-income demographic that the health community has traditionally underserved. We solve everyday problems for everyday people that are often overlooked by traditional tech companies.

What are the company's key accomplishments to date?

In under three years, we have contracted and been approved as a preferred vendor by large insurance companies and some of the most prestigious health systems across the country. Also, we have been able to drive meaningful outcomes and engagement, such as 80–90 percent compliance and a 52 percent smoking quit rate in our own comprehensive smoking cessation program. All this for a population that earns less than $20,000 on average. We have also conducted a successful clinical study with Boston Medical Center to prove viability among their most challenging in-patient population. To date, we have touched the lives of over 1,600 patients.

What lies ahead for Vincere?

We are starting around the single vertical of smoking cessation. However, we will ultimately focus on complex individual needs like low-income pregnant women and people with behavioral health comorbidities. There are a lot of needs these populations might have where we believe we can affect change. We plan to address mental and behavioral health needs across the country as well.

When people think about the most impactful companies in America improving the health of Medicaid populations, we want to be right at the top of that list. We are bringing cutting-edge technology to underserved populations through partnerships that we forge with various payers and providers. We won't be able to do this alone.

RON'S TAKE

Looking from the outside, it is all too easy to dismiss smoking and other addictions as "someone else's problem." Little consideration is given to the intrinsic reasons why certain populations, particularly those of a lower-income demographic, pick up smoking and other unhealthy lifestyle behaviors in the first place. Smoking, like any other addiction, can be extremely difficult to break out of. If one does not have the right motivations, monitoring, and human support to keep one on track, it becomes a vicious and virtually impossible cycle to break.

Such addictions also have an impact beyond that one person. Families and friends pay a price, and society at large often must make up the financial cost in the end, not to mention absorbing the additional strain on limited healthcare resources. Vincere Health is taking an innovative approach to counsel people to implement the changes that they seek for better health and wellness. The company's model relies on the payers, including government and private insurers, to accept the notion that an ounce of prevention is worth a pound of cure. Let's hope that more such institutions see both the financial and moral value of partnering with companies like Vincere working to make sure that the individuals who are trying to quit smoking have a viable, proven path to doing so.

Disclaimer: Alumni Ventures invested in the seed round of Vincere Health in mid-2021.

CREDA HEALTH

Creda Health (formerly KnowYourMeds) operates a digital health application intended to build a comprehensive database of medicines and their side effects for patients. The company's application offers pill reminders, prescription refills, and updates about the latest FDA regulations, enabling patients to prevent adverse reactions from either taking prescription medication without knowing its after-effects or forgetting to take them in the first place.

Headquarters and year founded: Waltham, MA, 2017
Founder: Kim Shah was most recently the global director of marketing for the informatics software business within Thermo Fisher Scientific, a $20 billion company empowering their customers to make a cleaner, healthier, and safer world.

During his career, Shah held executive-level positions at numerous high-tech companies, such as Inso Corporation, Lotus Development, and Micrografx. He is a marketing executive with a demonstrated impact in the research industry. He's a graduate of Imperial College London and holds an MBA from MIT's Sloan School of Management.

Funds raised and VC investors: $4 million from Innospark and angels.

Q&A WITH THE FOUNDER

Where did the idea for Creda Health originate?

I co-founded the company four years ago alongside our chairman, Venkat Srinivasan. We wanted to do something big from an impact and mission point of view. We looked at health as a massive area for technology disruption. A lot of us suffer from chronic conditions. Between doctor visits, however, most of the responsibility that we have for our own health relies on the action that we take. We didn't see people doing enough here in the U.S. that focused on this, let alone in the rest of the world, such as India and Africa.

What's the key problem that Creda Health intends to solve?

We wanted to address this gap with a platform that follows symptoms, vital signs, medication, and adherence. People have to worry about blood pressure, weight, and many other factors. Devices are available now to help, along with proper food and nutrition guidelines. With that in our mind, we started the journey with medicine first. People fundamentally don't know about drug interactions and side effects. We started looking at this from a data point of view due to the giant lack of information that patients have.

How are you most differentiated as a service?

We first built a giant database of 250,000 drug names, including brand-name and generic, and active ingredients. We gathered data available from user reports from the FDA and WHO and ended up with 50 million records. This was pretty messy to sort through, but we launched version one in October

2019 as a free app that was downloadable from anywhere. A user downloads the app, puts in their current drugs, including prescription and over-the-counter (OTC), and we start feeding back any available information on contraindications, foods to avoid, etc.

We realized this tended to be a one-and-done user experience. Users wouldn't come every day. In our next phase, we started using AI to determine what people's chronic conditions might be, based on the drugs they were taking. We considered gender, age, and other factors to share with users what they should be thinking about, such as scheduling colonoscopies and mammograms. We follow official guidance from public health authorities. The platform is meant to show "what you can do" about your health for those who care to stay diligent.

What are your key accomplishments to date?

We have around 60,000 active users on the app, of which two-thirds are in the U.S., nearly a third in India, plus a smattering in 100 other countries.

What lies ahead for Creda Health?

We are not going to be just about medications. In India, the skill level of medical practitioners ranges from the Harvard-trained doctor in Mumbai to the witch doctor in a village. We plan to bring the ability for a nurse-level provider to ask relevant diagnostic questions. We put the patient in touch with the right doctor. We make the process more efficient.

Most people in India are simply given antibiotics or antihistamines to treat their problems. We will offer a more comprehensive intervention by building an ecosystem of available specialists and a chat function using AI. We will connect patients with human nutritionists, pharmacists, physical therapists, may even psychiatrists. We have already contracted with many of these providers and will become a gig economy platform over time.

From a business standpoint, we plan to solve the black hole of what happens to patients when they are not at the clinic by helping clinics "keep an eye" on them. We have started working with a GI clinic, for example, to monitor IBD, Crohn's, Colitis, and soon other areas as well. We will do so through a revenue partnership with the clinics. We expect to have 20 clinics working with us by the end of the year and are in active discussions with some larger groups of clinics.

We also work directly with patients with diseases like diabetes and hypertension, and we target having 10,000 direct subscribers on the platform by the end of this year and one million by 2025.

From a social impact point of view, we feel that we can serve hundreds of millions of people. We have a relationship in India with a company called Karma Health that will vastly extend our reach. In rural India, some people don't have the literacy to understand the information we are asking for and subsequently providing. The solution is nurse-augmented telehealth. A villager comes to a clinic with a problem, and a nurse does the triage. From there, a telehealth visit is conducted with a doctor. Karma Health does the human part, but our business at Creda Health will be to manage the app and other technology, including AI-driven diagnostics.

From the revenue side, this can easily become a $100 million business or more. It won't all come from subscribers. If we show positive results at the clinic, reimbursements from insurers will become a real possibility. Then this becomes far more powerful. The other side is our AI engine. If we really develop it to be as powerful as we think we can, then there are additional areas with huge potential.

Medication is often more art than science. Practitioners don't know what medicine or dosage will work the best right away. It may need to be adjusted based on trial and error. Dosage may be different for one person versus another based on nationality and other classes of people. We intend to be able to recommend to clinicians with our data and AI what could work best.

RON'S TAKE

It has become almost cliché to say that healthcare ought to be a basic human right for all people anywhere in the world, no matter what their socioeconomic status, nationality, age, gender, ethnic, or racial background. And yet we are so far from this goal that it is almost incomprehensible.

Entrepreneurs such as Kim Shah and Venkat Srinivasan are rethinking what tools are possible through the application of AI and mobile technology to get every person basic information and access to treatment and prevention.

They have used their Western education, experience, and strong professional networks to move quickly toward bringing healthcare to those who lack what many of us take for granted. With additional funding and partnerships, the Creda Health model can have a significant impact across the world, where many still lack access to the information to help them monitor their health.

OLIVA

Oliva is well-being platform for companies that want to care for their employees and see them thrive. By combining coaching, dedicated support for managers, and mental fitness classes, all led by a curated team of top professionals, Oliva equips employees to handle whatever life throws at them at work and beyond. All services are completely free for employees, to ensure that they can focus on getting better without the burden of payment.

Headquarters and year founded: Barcelona & London, 2019

Founder: Javier Suarez, co-founder and CEO, is a serial entrepreneur whose previous startup, TravelPerk, has become a "unicorn" and one of the leading enterprise travel management SaaS platforms in the world. Javier is both a product- and mission-driven founder who started Oliva to help make mental healthcare more accessible and affordable for all. Previously, Javier worked on the innovation team at Booking.com. Fluent in English, Spanish, and German, Javier holds degrees from Touro College Berlin and the University of Navarra in Spain.

Funds raised and VC investors: $8.6 million from Moonfire Ventures, Start Capital, Stride.VC, and angel investors.

Q&A WITH THE FOUNDER

Where did the idea for Oliva originate?

Oliva started from a personal problem. At the first company I started, I had severe anxiety around year three. I didn't know what I was getting myself into as the company was growing bigger, and I had more responsibility to shoulder. I saw five different therapists around 2018, and after a year of trying, I finally found one that clicked for me. It made no sense that I had to go through a year of hoops to find the proper mental health care that I needed.

What's the key problem that Oliva intends to solve?

There is enough science in the world on how mental healthcare can help people. What is needed is to make it more accessible for people to reach that existing science. Other digital mental health companies are trying to use AI to come up with new ways of treating patients. However, we don't need new science. We need to make it easier to apply existing science.

We make it easy for employees and employers to maintain a healthy culture and well-being. Fifty percent of sick days are attributed to mental health. Human resource organizations develop recruitment, hiring, training, and retention practices. However, more often than not, companies leave their more important assets—brains—up to chance. The cost, if ignored, is massive in terms of sick days and unproductive work time. We make it easy for organizations to implement, measure, and create personalized journeys for what employees they need.

How are you most differentiated as a service?

We are differentiated in a number of ways:

We have made in-house care the highest priority. We have a chief clinical officer and a care model, not a marketplace. We want to be accountable. We take our patient-therapist matching seriously based on symptoms, as well as our care delivery. Everything is based on science. Our underlying care model brings an experienced in-house care team that is accountable for end results. We offer top-quality, robust care with clinical outcomes.

We are creating a company that focuses on a robust top line as well as bottom line that will operate and continue to be successful regardless of whether we raise more money from VCs. Our company is built for the long term.

We go deep in various types of care to suit different needs, including 1-to-1, 1-to-many, and self-help, and we combine these to create personalized journeys.

Our brand aims to de-stigmatize mental health and to help people feel encouraged and motivated to seek care.

The mission is to have company-wide impact by offering our services to leadership, middle management, and line employees alike.

What are the company's key accomplishments to date?

Oliva has helped over 2,500 people so far in the U.K., France, Germany, and Spain get the mental health care they seek. Many of these people would not have had the budget for therapy or counseling, but we eliminate the cost friction by working with employers. In the U.K., the "reliable improvement rate" for mental health patients is around 50 percent. However, we have already delivered at 70 percent, well above the national average.

What lies ahead for Oliva?

We have a lot of initiatives in different stages of development. First and foremost, we want to become the leading provider in Europe and the U.K. We plan to double down on different types of care and modalities while maintaining a high level of reliable improvement. We are currently providing services in seven languages and plan to add three more languages per quarter. We also hope to add family members to the employer plans in the future, and eventually, we expect to donate free help to people who are in need.

RON'S TAKE

If there is any aspect of healthcare that is in dire need of being made more affordable, more accessible, and de-stigmatized all at once, it is mental health care. Thankfully, forward-thinking organizations are starting to realize the benefit and significance of providing mental health services to their employees. As Peter Drucker once said, "Culture eats strategy for breakfast." Without healthy mindsets and well-being within an organization, it can be impossible to create a viable and thriving culture. Oliva is paving the way in Europe for normalizing high-quality mental health as an employee benefit, open to all without respect to one's means or job title. As services like Oliva are adopted en masse, it will become clear that we are entering a new era of companies putting their employees' emotional and psychological needs at the forefront.

Disclaimer: I previously co-founded TravelPerk alongside Javier and invested with personal funds in the pre-seed round of Oliva in July 2021.

ZÓCALO HEALTH

Zócalo Health provides a health-tech platform designed to improve the experience of accessing healthcare services and social benefits for the Latino population. The company provides a technology-enabled approach paired with in-person services, enabling clients to make accessing healthcare simple.

Headquarters and year founded: Seattle, 2021

Founder: Erik Cardenas, co-founder and CEO, is a healthcare technology strategist with over twenty years of experience in the industry. He founded Zócalo Health in August 2021 to deliver a first-class family medicine experience for the Latino community. Prior to this, he served as a senior manager at Amazon Care, where he oversaw several technical teams and programs. In March 2021, he was appointed to the Rogers Behavioral Health board of directors. Erik graduated with a BSBA in marketing and information systems from the University of the Incarnate World.

Funds raised and VC investors: $10 million from Able Partners, ANIMO Ventures, Great Oaks Venture Capital, Necessary Ventures, Vamos Ventures, Virtue VC.

Q&A WITH THE FOUNDER

Where did the idea for Zócalo Health originate?

I was born to Mexican immigrant parents and grew up in inner-city Houston, where I didn't have the best access to care or education. I was the first in my family to get into a major university and the first in my family to get kicked out of college (although I later completed college as an adult).

After leaving Texas A&M University, I got into the healthcare IT industry, first at Tenet Health and then as one of the first employees of Everlywell. Later on, I became the only Latino on the Amazon Care leadership team.

When the pandemic started, I was a key contributor to Amazon's broader Covid response which involved presenting a plan to Jeff Bezos and the rest of the S-Team. I was thriving and at the top of my career. However, the Covid experience really brought to light for me the disparities in healthcare equity in our society. Due to my background, I had a particular eye on the needs of the Latino community. So in August 2021, I resigned from Amazon, and the following month, I raised $3 million to start Zócalo Health with the mission to make healthcare more accessible and affordable for the U.S. Latino population.

What's the key problem that Zócalo Health intends to solve?

We exist to strengthen the health and well-being of the Latino community by eliminating barriers to accessing high-quality healthcare services with transparent pricing. Zócalo Health offers same-day virtual healthcare appointments and healthcare navigation assistance for a flat rate monthly membership fee.

For a greater impact on people's lives, "our care will extend beyond the confines of the physician's exam room. We will introduce the Latino community to a long overdue, improved experience that is built on trust, community, and a holistic approach that enables members to achieve optimal social, mental, and physical well-being. It is a tireless pursuit that will improve the lives of our patients and will build sustainable, healthier communities."[32]

How are you most differentiated as a service?

While new models of care are emerging and telehealth adoption has increased during the pandemic, a gap remains in the market for a trusted brand designed specifically for the Latino population to access convenient and high-quality primary care services. Language-based disparities in telehealth further restrict access for people with limited English proficiency who need care. While many market entrants have introduced virtual services like Zócalo Health, we see the main competition as the status quo of using brick-and-mortar services, FQHCs, or the Emergency Room. The lack of targeted telehealth services that seek to establish primary care relationships within population signals a need for Zócalo Health.

What are the company's key accomplishments to date?

We launched our beta in California in July and, so far, have enrolled over 100 patients. We launched Texas in September and will add the state of Washington before the end of the year. In addition, we have put together a winning team and have the infrastructure in place for our go-to-market strategy. In addition, we recently topped up the initial capital that we raised with a further $2 million to enable our market entry across multiple states.

What lies ahead for Zócalo Health?

Zócalo Health is building a primary care brand and experience for the Latino population in the U.S. Our approach to scale is broken down into three phases: first, focus on the experience of delivering high-quality direct-to-consumer care and patient acquisition; second, build out a brick and click (virtual services paired with in-person services) to add additional services for our members, and lastly, offer this community population health and risk management.

In order to scale to a fully value-based care company, we must first build the foundation of a strong, trusted brand that delivers culturally relevant care and removes existing barriers to access. Each of our three phases is designed to bring value to customers while helping to scale Zócalo Health into a risk-bearing entity.

RON'S TAKE

Disparities in healthcare access, quality, and affordability are not a new phenomenon; however, the depth of the problems has been illuminated further in recent years in part due to Covid's impact on underserved communities.

The large and fast-growing U.S. Latino community is notable for the lack of attention it has received from the health system in addressing shortcomings.

While still very early in its development, Zócalo Health offers a promising platform that marries digital with in-person care, according to the cultural needs of the diverse Latino population across the United States. Erik Cardenas brings an impressive Horatio Alger-style back story to his position as an entrepreneur who now hopes to empower more people in his community to obtain the level of healthcare that all humans deserve.

10

IMMIGRATION AND MIGRANT WORKERS

Despite the efforts of some politicians to paint a different picture, apart from our indigenous peoples who arrived here roughly 16,000 years ago (some experts say it could have been 37,000 years ago), the United States is a nation of immigrants. And while the stream of newcomers never ceased from the early days of the 16th century, today's immigrant composition of the United States really began with the 1965 Immigration Act. As NPR noted, prior to the passage of that law, "only about 4 percent of our population was foreign-born" and they came mostly from Europe. "By 2000, the share of the U.S. population born outside the country had risen to about 13 percent, with nine out of ten immigrants coming from countries outside Europe," making the United States the multicultural nation that it is today.[33]

The economic and societal benefits of immigration are almost too numerous to mention. They fill vital and often hard-to-fill jobs in the fields of manufacturing, farming, logistics, transportation, education, and countless types of service professions. They are also consumers, contributing $1.3 trillion in spending to the U.S. economy in 2019. Immigrants also pursue STEM careers in disproportionate numbers. "Foreign-born innovators are responsible for more than 75 percent of patents from the top ten patent-producing U.S. universities, according to New American Economy".[34] Moreover, immigrants have been awarded 38 percent of the Nobel Prizes won by Americans in chemistry, medicine, and physics since 2000, according to the National Foundation for American Policy. "Between 1901 and 2021, immigrants have been awarded

35 percent, or 109 of 311, of the Nobel Prizes won by Americans in chemistry, medicine and physics."[35]

Immigrants are most certainly an entrepreneurial bunch as well. While they make up approximately one-in-seven U.S. residents and one-in-six workers, they create a remarkable one in four new businesses, according to U.S. Census Bureau statistics and analysis conducted by professors Sari Kerr of Wellesley College and William Kerr, Unit Head of Entrepreneurial Management at Harvard Business School.[36]

These businesses are not merely mom-and-pop or solopreneur businesses. A July 2022 study by the National Foundation for American Policy revealed that fully 55 percent of American "unicorn" companies were founded by immigrants. There's SpaceX, Stripe, Instacart, Epic Games, and Gopuff, just to name a few.[37]

All of these phenomenal contributions notwithstanding, challenges faced by immigrants to America—or indeed to any nation—include language barriers, which can also amplify the effects of other sources of disadvantage; lack of employment opportunities and job discrimination; difficulties finding housing; poor access to healthcare services; arranging transportation, especially car ownership and drivers' licenses; differences of culture; and of course, plain old prejudice and the difficulty of being branded an outsider.

Migrant workers who come to the U.S. specifically to send money home face their own set of challenges. It's a big flow of money—according to the World Bank, in 2022, the total value of remittances sent by some 200 million migrant workers worldwide to their homes in low- and middle-income countries (LMICs) was $626 billion. "Immigrant workers depend on a multitude of remittance methods, providers, intermediaries, agents, and channels to provide financial support to their families every month."[38] According to the Remittances Prices Worldwide Database, in 2022, the cost of sending $200 across international borders to LMICs remained high at 6 percent on average. While mobile operators bring this cost lower on average, these channels are still yet to penetrate a meaningful share of the market. "The burden of compliance with Anti-Money Laundering/Combating the Financing of Terrorism (AML/CFT) regulations continues to restrict access of new service providers to correspondent banks and affect migrants' access to digital remittance services."[39] Below are several companies working to ease the financial and social burdens placed on immigrants and migrant workers.

BOUNDLESS

Boundless operates an online platform that empowers families to navigate the immigration system confidently, rapidly, and affordably. The company's platform provides United States immigrants with the tools, information, and personalized support to navigate their immigration journey, enabling clients to access immigration lawyers and file online.

Headquarters and year founded: Seattle, 2017

Founder: Xiao Wang, co-founder and CEO, started Boundless in 2017, having been an immigrant to the U.S. from China as a youth. His prior work experience includes senior product management experience at Amazon, portfolio operations at Providence Equity Partners, innovation and design at the NYC Department of Education, and consulting at McKinsey. He holds bachelor's and master's degrees in management science, engineering, and economics from Stanford, as well as an MBA from Harvard.

Funds raised and VC investors: $44 million from Alumni Ventures, AME Cloud Ventures, Emerson Collective, Escalate Capital Partners, Forefront Venture Partners, Founders' Co-op, Foundry Group, Industry Ventures, Pioneer Square Labs, Ride Ventures, The Graduate Syndicate, The Gramercy Fund, Trilogy Equity Partners, Two Sigma Ventures.

Q&A WITH THE FOUNDER

Where did the idea for Boundless originate?

As an immigrant, I personally and through my community have felt the struggles of immigration for decades. Like most other immigrants, I took these struggles for granted or as a rite of passage that every immigrant has to go through. We assume the pains along this journey. But in 2016 I met someone who spent $12,000 on an immigration attorney for a green card application and had a very bad experience. It was then that I asked the question of "why" for the first time. Once I started asking this question, it became clear that the process is an immense problem that is solvable. This shouldn't have to be this way. The immigration process hasn't changed in generations. It takes advantage of folks without resources. The process itself keeps people from being with their loved ones and living the life that they want to lead. I grew convinced that there was no way that I couldn't *not* try to solve this.

What's the key problem that Boundless intends to solve?

At the core, immigration is hard because of the huge information gap and the high stakes involved in petitioning the U.S. government. Getting this wrong can result in a person being deported and sent away from loved ones. It can mean not being able to work, travel, study, or live life as one would want.

At the same time, there is a dearth of information for one to know if they are completing their applications correctly. People are caught between the tradeoff of spending thousands of dollars on lawyer fees (even though many immigrants are not able to work yet) or trying to figure this out on one's own and struggling, not knowing for weeks or months if they have done it correctly.

Because of this information gap and insecurity around properly completing applications, there are now roughly ten times as many immigration attorneys as when I came to this country 30 years ago, even though the actual number of immigrants has not increased to such a degree.

This is the kind of problem that technology and data are meant to solve. We take everything that's in the minds of government officials who review immigration documents, and we make the application process accessible and affordable to everyone.

How are you most differentiated as a service?

We have become the largest processor of U.S. immigration documents. We process more than any lawyer, and we start by building trust. We are the most visited website for immigration outside of the U.S. government. We offer the highest quality resources and guides for the immigration process available on the Internet. In the past, people had to go around the Internet searching for information. We have been quoted by news services and members of Congress in immigration reform proposals.

By shining light in a black box, we prioritize the user experience. An experience that took weeks and months previously can now be done in a couple of hours. Most people don't ask to understand all of the forms and questions, so we translate this into something that normal people can understand. We help guide people through this journey. There is also a flywheel as the more families we help, it becomes increasingly clearer that we are the best option. We do more than everyone else and have insights on timing and written and unwritten rules that adjudicators look for in applications. We offer the best experience available.

What are the company's key accomplishments to date?

Boundless has helped over 73,000 people successfully get their immigration paperwork done. We have achieved a 99.97 percent success rate in the applications we've helped to submit. Although we are the most visited U.S. immigration website outside of the U.S. government, we are just scratching the surface of the opportunity. Our goal is to become the default choice across all immigrant communities.

What lies ahead for Boundless?

We got started by offering marriage green cards, then naturalization, then children, fiancée, and parents. We acquired RapidVisa last year and expanded into parent green cards and travel visas, and we are actively looking at additional areas of expansion around the entire immigration stack. We chose the name Boundless for a reason—to help people not only get into the U.S. but to thrive in their first ten years in the country. We aim to be able to help with every case in immigration eventually. When my family came over and moved to Tempe, Arizona, we just asked a Chinese family that had already been settled for a few years how to do things like get a car, a bank account, and buy a house. There was no other good way. I believe we can do so much better than that.

We want to make it irresponsible for immigrants not to be a member of Boundless. Our goal is to help improve life so much that every immigrant has an affiliation with Boundless.

Most immigration cases are family-based. It's not just H-1Bs. A third of our customers are within 25 percent of the poverty line. For them, they've historically gotten no help or have been taken advantage of with unscrupulous or unqualified help. Through the Boundless network, we can do things for families that have not been readily available. For green card families, people often need to apply before even getting a work permit. It costs $1,760 to apply, which is a lot for most people, let alone people who can't work. We offer no credit check financing and can create payment plans for U.S. government fees. Without this, some immigrants would need to resort to payday lender rates or have no access to financing at all. We help with all steps in this process. We open up different avenues. Our mission is to empower our members to rise up and achieve things their parents or grandparents could never do.

RON'S TAKE

"Give me your tired, your poor, your huddled masses yearning to breathe free…as long as they can afford thousands of dollars in legal fees, of course!"

Legal immigration has made the United States what it is today. Immigrants are well documented to be highly entrepreneurial, fill critical skill gaps in the economy, and overall added $2 trillion to U.S. GDP in 2016. Never mind the contributions that immigrants make to education, science, medicine, the arts, culture, cuisine, and everything else that makes this a wonderful country. These contributions are recognized across the geographic and socioeconomic spectrum of immigrants.

Boundless is in the business of empowering these immigrants to achieve their legal status in this country without facing the often-prohibitive costs for many families of obtaining this. Combining technology, human involvement, and collective experience and expertise, Xiao and his team will clear the pathway for families who desire to settle and contribute to this country in a way that is easier on the nerves and friendlier to the wallet.

Disclaimer: Alumni Ventures invested in the Series B round of Boundless in spring 2021.

BOLDVOICE

BoldVoice is a mobile application for non-native English speakers. The app helps to improve English language pronunciation and confidence via personalized content from Hollywood accent coaches and instant feedback from speech AI, enabling foreign-born professionals and students in the U.S. to improve their English accents and advance their careers.

Headquarters and year founded: New York, 2020

Founder: Anada Lakra is a native of Albania who came to the U.S. to study at Yale and has since blazed a trail as a management consultant at McKinsey and as a product manager at several leading technology companies, including Peloton. Anada also received her MBA from Harvard Business School.

Funds raised and VC investors: $3 million from Flybridge Capital, Liquid2 Ventures, XFund, Y Combinator, and angel investors.

Q&A WITH THE FOUNDER

Where did the idea for BoldVoice originate?

The idea of BoldVoice is based on my own lived experience as an immigrant. When I moved to the U.S. for college, I experienced the pain of having studied English for years but then suddenly struggling to speak conversationally among native speakers. I was often asked to repeat myself. Not being able to be properly understood is a nearly universal problem for immigrants. My co-founder Ilya Usorov, whose parents immigrated from Russia, aced these challenges at work and felt the impact of their foreign accent on their career advancement.

When I was attending HBS, I again saw international students struggle to speak up in class and feel confident during job interviews, even though they spoke English fluently "on paper." All these experiences inspired me to do something about this unaddressed problem that so many experience.

What's the key problem that BoldVoice intends to solve?

Studies have shown that an accent can make job candidates 16 percent less likely to be hired, and entrepreneurs are 23 percent less likely to be able to raise money for their businesses. We want to help immigrants and non-native speakers always be understood and confident in English so that they can overcome these barriers.

The inspiration for this business was a friend who was able to gain confidence in speaking by hiring a professional accent coach. I didn't even know it was possible to get coaching for speech; the problem was it cost $200 an hour for one session. That is when I had a "lightbulb moment." Through technology, I knew that this solution could be automated to serve the vast market of those who simply couldn't afford $200 per hour lessons.

How are you most differentiated as a service?

Our vision was to build an experience that is as effective as working one-on-one with a speech and accent coach yet affordable and accessible. We needed a scalable technology product to do this. We started by working with Hollywood accent coaches and produced video lessons for people of different linguistic backgrounds. This allowed us to offer "personalization at scale" by serving our users with only relevant content based on their challenges from their mother tongue.

Our speech AI layer provides instant feedback and mimics what coaches would give as one-on-one feedback in a private session. The speech AI is precise enough to catch small differences in pronunciation. The combination of our coaching and video content is highly effective in helping our users feel improvement in every session on the app.

What are the company's key accomplishments to date?

Today we serve hundreds of thousands of users who speak over 90 native languages across all different linguistic backgrounds. We offer hundreds of video lessons from six Hollywood accent coaches and a myriad of practice materials. Our user base has been growing multi-fold in just the past six months, with users all around the world.

What lies ahead for BoldVoice?

We have found a lot of user love, and we are going to continue building our product to serve more people. We will also be pursuing additional growth channels to help us get in front of more people. We are currently focused on attracting immigrants in the U.S. However, we also plan on global expansion, especially targeting those who work for multinational or American companies globally. The long-term vision is to help every non-native English speaker access better professional opportunities through clear and confident communication in the language of business.

RON'S TAKE

Immigrants to the U.S. are an incredibly powerful and well-documented source of social, economic, and cultural capital and diversity. Since this country's inception, this has always been the case, and it makes us who we are. Yet immigrants too often face barriers and burdens that most of us do not even stop to consider. As Boundless is helping immigrants manage the cost and complexity of entering and settling in the United States, BoldVoice is tackling one of the other most important gaps, which is the ability for newcomers to integrate into educational, professional, and social settings in the country by being able to communicate and be understood more clearly.

CASHEX

CashEx offers a digital banking platform for African migrants that provides essential financial tools before, during, and after migration.

Headquarters and year founded: Boston, 2022
Founder: Kingsley Ezeani, co-founder and CEO, is an entrepreneur with 12 years of experience building and scaling technology businesses in Africa. He is a Mid-Career Master in Public Administration candidate at

Harvard Kennedy School and a graduate of the Oxford MBA program. In 2019, Kingsley was selected as an Obama Foundation African Leader.

Funds raised and VC investors: $750,000 from Pillar VC, angel investors, and grants.

Q&A WITH THE FOUNDER

Where did the idea for CashEx originate?

Having been an immigrant from Nigeria to the U.K. and U.S., I have witnessed the difficulties immigrants face in obtaining basic banking and other financial services such as remittances. Africans are among the largest populations of immigrants currently (with 110,000 African migrants to the U.S. each year), but there are few digital banking services that are fitting their needs. As an entrepreneur who previously founded one of the largest media businesses in Nigeria, I felt it was my next mission to create a platform that would empower this community with the financial services that they need.

What's the key problem that CashEx intends to solve?

We plan to solve several problems for African migrants: saving U.S. dollars in Africa (as a hedge against currency devaluation), opening bank accounts in the U.S. to help with savings and establishing credit, and sending money back to Africa, which has some of the highest remittance fees in the world.

How are you most differentiated as a service?

We work with migrants before, during, and after their journey from Africa to the U.S. (and later, to Europe). Our digital-first platform allows us to acquire users before they emigrate abroad seamlessly. Once we launch our remittance service, we will also dramatically reduce the cost of sending money back home.

What are the company's key accomplishments to date?

We have had 50,000 sign-ups so far in just two months since launching in beta. Over 4,000 users have tried our U.S. dollar savings product. We are also proud to have won awards from the Harvard Business School New Venture Competition, the Harvard President's Innovation Challenge, as well as new venture forums at MIT. We also got funded by Google as part of the Google Black Founder's Fund.

What lies ahead for CashEx?

We plan to launch our digital bank in the U.S. by March 2023 and our remittance product by Q4. Our goal is to stretch beyond Nigeria and the U.S. to become the digital banking platform of choice for all African migrants worldwide.

RON'S TAKE

We have explored the plight of immigrants of migrant workers previously with companies such as Boundless and BoldVoice. Often among the most overlooked members of society, immigrants are ironically among the most productive and additive to the economic and cultural engines of their new homeland. Millions of native Africans now call the U.S. home, and this number is only going to increase.

CashEx will enable them to not only integrate more easily into society but also to earn and return more of their hard-earned dollars to family members back home who live off meager incomes. Rather than being treated as second-class citizens or ignored entirely, immigrants should receive a red-carpet welcome, and innovative fintech companies like CashEx will play a critical role in doing so.

TANGAPP

TANGapp provides a peer-to-peer international mobile payment platform that allows migrant workers to send money home in a manner that is convenient and much lower cost than existing alternatives.

Headquarters and year founded: New York, 2020

Founder: Rebecca Kersch, founder and CEO, started TANGapp following several years working at Saïd Business School of Oxford University. She has also been a management consultant with Strategy& and has worked in field strategy with the United Nations. Rebecca has lived in several countries across the globe and is a graduate of Vrije Universiteit Amsterdam, the University of Sydney, the Rotterdam School of Management, and the Harvard Kennedy School.

Funds raised and VC investors: $1.5 million in pre-seed funding from grants, including the Harvard President's Innovation Challenge, MassChallenge, and seventeen angels. Currently closing their seed round of $2.5 million, with investors including Goodwater, TEN13, and Visible Hands.

Q&A WITH THE FOUNDER

Where did the idea for TANGapp originate?

I am Filipino, Dutch, and American. I grew up in the Netherlands but went to the Philippines every year. My aunt has always been a migrant worker who lived outside the Philippines and always sent money home by Western Union, which is what most migrants use. They pay an average of 8 percent of their pay to send money home. That means one month of every year's income goes just to cover Western Union fees. This has always struck me as exorbitant.

I went to do on-the-ground research in the Philippines and had a realization that the market needed a peer-to-peer payment app that would lower fees to migrant workers and give people in the Philippines access to better financial services. I then set about to create an international P2P mobile payment app, like Venmo, that would allow people to send money home and eventually have use for in-home and personal purchases as well.

What's the key problem that TANGapp intends to solve?

Our vision is that sending money should be as easy as texting. We are using the Philippines as a beachhead since it is a large market of 110 million people. An estimated $35 billion is sent home each year, accounting for 10 percent of the country's GDP. Global remittances are close to $590 billion. Many of these recipients are unbanked and therefore need more convenient and cost-effective solutions for sending and receiving money.

How are you most differentiated as a service?

We are building an international P2P mobile payment app that will allow transactions of as little as $5 to be sent from the U.S. to the Philippines, for example. We focus on micropayments of under $100 and are building a tool that brings together the best of Remitly, Wise, Venmo, and other cash apps. We are building a horizontal platform that will connect the $35 billion of remittances from the start to the end of the value chain. We have developed a payment rail setup that works with API partners to keep fees as low as possible.

What are the company's key accomplishments to date?

We grew in 2022 by over 35 percent month-on-month after our launch. Over 14,000 people have installed our app, and we have more than 40 percent repeat usage. We have big partnerships with charities in the Philippines. It's hard to get donations from the U.S., but donations can go through TANGapp for as little as $10. We have launched several products, grown to twelve people, and are now approved for remittance licenses in the Philippines and the United States.

What lies ahead in the plans for TANGapp?

We have some big product launches coming this year, and our plan is to grow our transaction volume by twenty times. The next big plan is to explore growth in another country.

RON'S TAKE

The plight of migrant workers is too often overlooked and downright dismissed. Frequently treated as second-class citizens, migrants very often do the critical low-wage jobs that natives to a country will not. They leave their homelands not to mooch off the largesse of others but to serve vital needs and to generate income that is quite often really to support their families back home. However, the simple act of sending what they earn back home is essentially "taxed" by a system of cash remittance intermediaries. This system is fully automated today by incumbent institutions operating the infrastructure behind these payments. And yet, what amounts to a one-month tax on yearly earnings is what migrants have to pay just to share their hard-earned money with loved ones back home who need the money for survival.

Disruptive companies like TANGapp are at the forefront of reducing these financial burdens. In the process, they are making remittances faster and easier for all. More migrant workers providing services will benefit both the country where they arrive to work and the people back home who have fewer opportunities for economic advancement. Migrants must be rewarded rather than penalized for the hard work and sacrifices that they endure. TANGapp is helping migrants to make one important step forward.

11

DISABILITY TECHNOLOGY

Before the Americans with Disabilities Act of 1990 (ADA) was passed, employers could set the conditions under which they would hire an individual with a disability. For example, if you used a wheelchair or some other ambulatory tool and you applied for a job, an employer could simply say, "Sorry, we don't think you could handle it," and toss your application into the trash. No explanation was needed, and no accommodation was required.

While the Civil Rights Act of 1964 had made discrimination based on race, religion, sex, national origin, and other characteristics illegal—later including sexual orientation and gender identity—the ADA broadened the scope of protected classes by requiring employers to ensure reasonable accommodations were available for employees with disabilities and imposing accessibility requirements on public accommodations.

As defined by the ADA, a person with a disability is someone who:

- Has a physical or mental impairment that substantially limits one or more major life activities, or
- Has a history or record of such an impairment (such as cancer that is in remission), or
- Is perceived by others as having such an impairment (such as a person who has scars from a severe burn).

If a person falls into any of these categories, the ADA protects them.

Aside from mobility disabilities such as those requiring the use of a wheelchair, walker, or cane, specific diseases or conditions that may qualify as a disability include autism, blindness or low vision, cancer, deafness, diabetes, HIV, post-traumatic stress disorder, and many more.

The ADA's influence over employers has opened a new world of employment possibilities for people with a wide range of disabilities and encourages employers to tap into a source of previously hidden talent.

For entrepreneurs, the ADA created a new industry, assistive technology (AT), devoted to using technology to help people with disabilities take advantage of employment opportunities. And precisely because many disabled people are unemployed or underemployed, they need the help! As Sheryl Burgstahler reported in "The Role of Technology in Preparing Youth with Disabilities for Postsecondary Education and Employment," individuals with disabilities are "less than half as likely as their non-disabled counterparts to own computers, and they are about one-quarter as likely to use the Internet... Office equipment that cannot be operated from a seated position is inaccessible to an employee who uses a wheelchair for mobility," just to name a few examples.[40]

The Assistive Technology Industry Association (ATIA) defines assistive technology as "any item, piece of equipment, software program, or product system that is used to increase, maintain, or improve the functional capabilities of persons with disabilities... Assistive technology helps people who have difficulty speaking, typing, writing, remembering, pointing, seeing, hearing, learning, walking, and many other things. Different disabilities require different assistive technologies."[41] AT can be very simple and low-tech or very complex, with the range including electronic devices, speech recognition software, wheelchairs, walkers, braces, educational software, power lifts, pencil holders, eye-gaze, head trackers, and much more. And according to the ADA, employers may be required to pay for AT that is a "reasonable accommodation" to enable an employee to perform essential job tasks.[42]

In addition, many emerging companies are focused on the applicant side, helping job seekers with disabilities to train for the jobs that are now available, and helping them navigate the application process so they can use their previously hidden talents in the workforce.

One investor who is dedicated to helping empower those with disabilities is Regina "Gina" Kline, managing partner of Enable Ventures, an impact fund that is backed by the Utah-based Sorenson Impact Group. A civil rights and disability rights lawyer who formerly worked in the Obama Administration, Gina teamed up with entrepreneur/investor Jim Sorenson, a pioneer in disability technology, to develop the first dedicated venture fund for disability technology. She believes the focus on work offers significant white space for innovation. As disability can be a spectrum, it turns out that 90 percent of those with a disability never inform their employer for fear of being judged unfit in some way to fulfill their duties. By working with many entrepreneurs who themselves have disabilities, Gina and her team at Enable Ventures aim to accelerate innovation that will make individuals with disabilities more productive workers and their employers better prepared to empower them.

DAIVERGENT

Daivergent is an online platform that offers professional training and employment placement that connects enterprise clients with people on the autism spectrum and with other disabilities. The offering is made available both directly to users as well as under contract with state governments.

Headquarters and year founded: New York, 2017

Founder: Byran Dai, co-founder and CEO, started Daivergent after having worked in the healthcare industry as a data scientist, consultant, and researcher. He has been affiliated with Massachusetts General Hospital, the Maryland Department of Health, and Johns Hopkins School of Public Health, as well as for-profit organizations such as Analysis Group and Quartet Health. Byran holds a bachelor's degree in history and science from Harvard University and a master's in epidemiology from Johns Hopkins University.

Byran founded Daivergent with CTO Rahul Mahida, who brought more than a decade of experience as a software engineer and web developer at both small and large enterprises in a variety of industries. Rahul attended Rockland Community College (NY) and Stevens Institute of Technology (NJ).

Funds raised and VC investors: $5.5 million from AEON Foundry, Divergent Investments, Emergence Capital Partners, Entrepreneurs Roundtable Accelerator, HBS Alumni Angels New York, Kapor Capital, New York Angels, On Grid Ventures, Remarkable Ventures Fund, SAP.iO, Western Technology Investment, Zeal Capital Partners.

Q&A WITH THE FOUNDER

Where did the idea for Daivergent originate?

Because my brother is on the autism spectrum, the challenges of neurodiversity have long been top of mind for me. When he turned 22, for instance, all he wanted was to find a job and live a normal, happy life. However, this can be much more difficult for those with autism and other disorders than one might realize. Having worked in the field of public health for a number of years, I needed to dedicate myself to developing solutions that would empower a workforce of those with autism and other disorders who could still contribute and be productive members of society.

What's the key problem that Daivergent intends to solve?

We provide vocational, social, and life skills training to those with autism and other forms of neurodiversity. Oftentimes they have very useful skills and talent but need help and guidance to secure and retain jobs, as well as developing additional skills for the future. Beyond offering this vital training, we also help our users to secure placement with employers who are understanding and enthusiastic to welcome them into their employee base. It is a win-win for both employee and employer. This program can also be funded by states, such as Arizona, which believe this to be a critical element of their workforce development.

How are you most differentiated as a service?

At Daivergent, we work with our users to develop personalized, lifelong plans. We are on the frontier of neurodiversity and are the first reimbursable program in the market. We offer coaching and, through job placement, are able to track the performance and satisfaction of our users and the employers who hire them.

What are the company's key accomplishments to date?

We are actively working with major employers such as Walmart and are approved for reimbursement with the state of Arizona. Texas will come next and will be followed by California, which is already in a demonstration phase. We are on plan to go to $4 million of ARR by serving 400 families per year. Furthermore, we are ready to launch in any state. We have developed proprietary content that is offered both in real time on a one-to-one basis, as well as asynchronously, with much of our content being reusable. To date, we have focused on training for jobs in IT, customer service, operations/administration, and graphic design.

What lies ahead for Daivergent?

Right now, we are focused on executing well in our Phase 1 launch states. Our first three states make up a quarter of the national potential. We are going to be tailored and adaptable but also be able to leverage asynchronous content to reach a much broader set of users. We look forward to changing the lives of thousands and eventually millions of families with autism and other disabilities.

RON'S TAKE

According to the Centers for Disease Control and Prevention, in the United States, one in four adults has some form of disability. Inequality is more acute in groups with less power and reduced ability to speak out. But having a disability should not be construed as being unable to be accomplished and productive for the benefit of oneself and society. The missing pieces are empowerment through education, training, mentoring, and sometimes therapy on one side, with empathy, resources, and opportunity on the other. The emerging category of innovation in "disability technology" hopes to change much of this. Daivergent is on the cutting edge of rethinking how we can address the gaps that will allow those on the autism spectrum and with other disabilities to reach their full human potential. All of society will reap the benefits of such productivity and accomplishment.

INCLUSIVELY

Inclusively provides a workforce inclusion platform that connects job seekers with employers who are committed to attracting and retaining previously hidden talent. The platform equips employers with the access, accommodation insights, support, and training they need.

Headquarters and year founded: Richmond, VA, 2019

Founder: Charlotte Dales, co-founder and CEO, is a serial entrepreneur who previously founded CAKE Technologies, which she sold to American Express, where she remained for several years and served as VP of benefit innovation. Charlotte previously worked as an investment banker with Deutsche Bank in London and New York. Charlotte holds a degree in media studies from the University of Colorado in Boulder.

Funds raised and VC investors: $5.5 million from Acumen America, Arch Grants, Charlottesville Angel Network, Eudaimonia Capital, How Women Invest, Naples Technology Ventures, Purple Sage Ventures, Sorenson Impact Foundation, Tech Square Ventures, The Pearl Fund.

Q&A WITH THE FOUNDER

Where did the idea for Inclusively originate?

I lived in London for ten years, where I started and sold my first company. At the same time, my cousin became the first known licensed facialist with Down's syndrome. Her employer only had to make slight adjustments to allow her to work in a professional environment. It's a rewarding career for her and more meaningful than simply folding towels.

I got to thinking about how to make it easier for employees across the disability spectrum. I thought about how to create a data model around personalization. The ADA sets what is a reasonable accommodation, but it allows for employer subjectivity and interpretation. My cousin was always encouraged by her parents to do more than other people would tell her she was capable of. People with disabilities should be empowered with the tools to have the most productive and rewarding careers possible.

What's the key problem that Inclusively intends to solve?

We are solving for people with disabilities by enabling them to access more professional positions. Historically people were told not to disclose disabilities for fear of ruining their chances in the hiring process. On the candidate side, we are giving more tools as well as access to employers. On the employer side, we solve the problem of being able to provide accommodations to people with a range of disabilities and scale up that capability. We're helping employers to operationalize ESG goals. We help with establishing accommodations, instruction, and training. The current solutions are not working, and we need to ensure people receive the information that they need. We are working with nonprofits, the Veterans Administration, and government agencies and aggregating into one place a pipeline of talent.

How are you most differentiated as a service?

On the candidate side, we work with them to upload credentials and information typical for job searching. We help them select relevant jobs and prepare for interviews while recommending candidates through our applicant tracking system.

On the employer side, we know what accommodations our candidates require. There are consultancies that have developed strategies, but these are typically made for executing in 10,000-person companies. Our biggest differentiator is that our solution actually helps everyone. We offer flexibility and equity while normalizing the ability to ask for accommodations and become more successful.

We can make the workforce more productive with a lower turnover rate and help the employer to make measurable progress.

What are the company's key accomplishments to date?

We work with over 50 enterprises, including Apple, Accenture, Delta Air Lines, Charles Schwab, and Barclays. We started with big companies, as this will make it easier to enter the mid-market. Our annual recurring revenue has now topped $1 million.

Our platform provides opportunities to one million candidates through 1,000 different advocate organizations. We use our network to target candidates to help place them in the right jobs. Over 50,000 active candidates use our platform across a wide range of jobs and geographies.

What lies ahead for Inclusively?

We are focused on getting employers more engaged while also adding as many people with an account as possible, similar to LinkedIn. We aim to be able to serve anyone. The tools that people with disabilities will use will be applicable for anyone. We aim to create true equity. As an additional next step, we will be looking to work directly with caregivers on the tools they require.

RON'S TAKE

Undervaluing and dismissing the potential of individuals with disabilities is a sad historical legacy that needs to be overcome. It begins with believing people should not be held back because of low expectations. The next step is to provide tools, resources, and a supportive community that will enable people with disabilities to contribute to their maximum potential. Employers play a huge role in this, not just by a willingness to hire more people but by being able to train and accommodate them. Organizations must practice what they preach around diversity and inclusion. Tools such as Inclusively will allow them to do this and even gain a competitive advantage against competitors who continue to look away from this untapped supply of talent.

VOICEITT

Voiceitt's speech recognition software provides voice accessibility systems for individuals with non-standard speech patterns. The software utilizes an AI-driven speech engine which can interpret non-standard speech, enabling customers who have motor, speech, and language disorders to easily communicate using their own voices by translating the unintelligible pronunciation into understandable speech.

Headquarters and year founded: Ramat Gan, Israel, 2012

Founders: Sara Smolley, co-founder and head of partnerships, joined Voiceitt's founding team in Israel after spending five years working and studying (MBA) in Hong Kong and South Korea. She has held various roles over the years in human resources, education, marketing, product management, and startup business development. Sara received a BA in economics from Barnard College (New York) and an MBA from Yonsei School of Management (South Korea).

Danny Weissberg, co-founder and CEO, has nearly two decades of experience in entrepreneurship, business development, management, innovation, research, and development in cutting-edge technologies of complex software solutions. He has spent more than ten years working as a software developer in AI and ML in the space of speech recognition and accessibility. Danny is a graduate of the Technion, Open University, and Tel Aviv University.

Dr. Stas Timokin, co-founder and CTO, is an assistant professor in computer engineering at San Jose State University. Previously, he was a postdoctoral researcher in the Robot Learning Lab of the Berkeley Artificial Intelligence Research at UC Berkeley. He received a PhD in computer science and engineering from Hebrew University in Jerusalem.

Funds raised and VC investors: $20 million in equity investment and grant funding. Institutional investors include AARP, the Amazon Alexa Fund, AMIT Technion, Cisco Investments, Connecticut Innovations, Dreamit Ventures, Microsoft M12, Quake Capital, and Techstars.

Q&A WITH THE CO-FOUNDER, SARA SMOLLEY

Where did the idea for Voiceitt originate?

All three of us who are part of the founding team of Voiceitt were inspired by personal experiences. Danny is a civil engineer turned impact entrepreneur. Stas is a former UC Berkeley postdoc who specializes in AI and natural language technology. I came to this because of my grandmother, who had early onset Parkinson's disease and lost the ability to speak and be understood when she was only in her forties. For Danny, this mission started when someone close to him lost the ability to communicate because of a stroke. He observed that caregivers learned ways of understanding him and other patients with similar speech deficiencies. He felt that if humans could figure out a way of understanding, then with enough data, machines could do so as well.

What's the key problem that Voiceitt intends to solve?

We create technology for in-person communication for individuals with speech impairments. We are like a Google Translate app that allows people to speak with medical professionals and say basic phrases, like when ordering a coffee. We do this on a personalized level by collecting voice samples and synthesizing speech. Because it is personalized, it can work in any language. One of the most important use cases is for voice-enabled smart home devices like Amazon Alexa. These devices can start to understand people with non-standard speech patterns through our Voiceitt translator, which operates "behind the scenes" in these devices.

How are you most differentiated as a service?

There is no better time to be in speech recognition. Having everything in the home become touchless and voice-activated is no longer science fiction. We have built an API and SDK that are easily integrated, flexible, and spontaneous. It takes minimum training time, and our technology is more powerful than standard language translation. For this reason, we are being approached by companies in a wide variety of verticals. We are partnering with wearable devices, for example, to become accessible to all consumers.

What are the company's key accomplishments to date?

We have had thousands of downloads of our app without any deliberate marketing. We believe the usefulness of the product speaks for itself. Demonstration videos are available on YouTube by searching for "Voiceitt."

What lies ahead for Voiceitt?

We will continue to be at the forefront of making voice technology inclusive. We have partnered with great strategic investors like Amazon, Microsoft, Cisco, and AARP, who recognize that designing products like this for anyone can eventually benefit everyone.

RON'S TAKE

Voiceitt is giving voice to those who need it, both literally and figuratively. What is technology here for, if not to solve real problems? People with disabilities are often among the most overlooked and dismissed in our society, and that is not just an indignity for them, but it is a loss for everyone. When one cannot communicate with others, they become disenfranchised and unable to live up to their potential. Voiceitt's technology is providing a monumental leap forward for a segment of the population that has been downplayed for far too long.

12

INCREASING CHARITABLE GIVING

P eople derive deep satisfaction from making monetary donations to the charities of their choice. Americans are generous; according to Giving USA, they gave a record $471 billion to charities in 2020.

Here are two statistics that may surprise you: Only a fraction (20 percent) of donations come from corporations, and individuals making less than $50,000 a year give more relative to total income than those in all other income ranges except the highest earners.

And two more from Define Financial: 2020 saw a massive 20 percent increase in online giving, with the average online donation being $177; and the *least* likely reason for people to give is so they can get a tax break.[43]

The Philanthropy Roundtable attributes this to three characteristics of American society and tradition: Americans have an entrepreneurial spirit and are ready to help others advance in life; a spirit of social consciousness; and a religious motivation (giving to one's church is a big part of charity).

Here's a statistic that many charities would like to tweak: The average age of the U.S. donor is 64, putting them squarely in the Baby Boomer generation. Here are some innovative companies finding ways to make charitable giving easier for people of all ages.

CAUZE

Cauze offers an app designed to allow individuals to create their own personal foundations, enabling them to give to any nonprofit, in any amount, from their phones. Cauze then leverages social dynamics to connect people around giving back. People can see when others give (never how much) and then "join" them by adding $1 or more instantly. This creates ripples of good that amplify as more people join. Anyone on the platform can match others, and on average, for every dollar donated, $2.50 goes to a nonprofit.

Headquarters and year founded: Boise, Idaho, 2017

Founder: Jason Hausske, founder and CEO, has led sales and business development at numerous venture-backed technology companies. He has long been interested in social impact and philanthropy, which led him to found Cauze. Jason holds a degree in economics from the University of Washington.

Funds raised and VC investors: $2 million from Acadian Ventures, Salmon Innovation Fund, ImpactAssets

Q&A WITH THE FOUNDER

Where did the idea for Cauze originate?

The idea came initially out of personal need. I felt like I personally should be giving more. I was inspired by charity websites and matched giving through retailers like Amazon and Whole Foods. I have wondered, though, how I could inspire a new wave of philanthropy where giving becomes a core part of one's identity?

What's the key problem that Cauze intends to solve?

There are multiple problems that we try to solve, but the primary one for individuals is "latent good," meaning the gap between charitable intent and action. Three hundred billion dollars are donated each year in the United

States. I believe people would give more if it fed their souls and connected them. Our core mission is to create a new world where people are empowered to give at those moments.

We also aim to attract and engage the next generation of donors. We hear from many employers who say that they want to better understand how to engage employees through purpose. The old rewards for employees don't seem to resonate. Brands want more meaningful engagement as well and seek a mechanism to engage. We follow groups that curate charities, such as the Obama Foundation, where someone can come with one donation that will then get split among many recipients. Our platform curates charities and allows people to give instantly and amplify any cause across multiple recipients.

How are you most differentiated as a service?

For the individual giver, the key is utility. Every donor gets the utility of a donor-advised fund combined with social connection and expression about the giver. Our giving platform also does not charge our individual donors. We monetize as a SaaS business offering to employers and brands looking for engaging, impactful solutions through offering matched funds.

What are the company's key accomplishments to date?

Historically donor-advised funds have been offered to wealthy people by firms like Fidelity and Schwab. We want to democratize this for everyone. Our platform has processed over $3 million in donations and has been used by 30,000 individuals thus far. Over 10,000 people have created accounts with us. From an impact perspective, every $1 donated has resulted in a 250 percent increase in the amount that goes to charity. In Cauze, we enable matching and the ability to join with others, a system where people increase their contributions organically. It is more consistent with how people interact in life. We believe that every donation should be social.

What lies ahead for Cauze?

We have a multi-sided platform and have been pulled in multiple directions. Our portal is being built for employers and nonprofits, but we want to get back to the heart of the app, which is the giver. We will offer improved onboarding, clarity, rewards, and premium paid accounts.

Every person in the U.S. will inevitably have a personal giving account, just like we have a checking account and savings account. We will become a social network, not just a bank that provides giving accounts as a tool. The idea is that we're all connected, and even kids will start with an account from a young age.

RON'S TAKE

From a young age, in my Jewish cultural tradition, we were brought up with the idea of *tzedakah*, which is essentially charity as a moral obligation and an act of social justice. Nearly everyone has causes that they believe in and would like to share and spread with others. Yet the idea of giving as a social or community activity has really not been enabled across philanthropy in a highly organized and accessible way. Cauze is leading the charge to change this by encouraging employees and employers to give and share with many worthy nonprofit organizations. By democratizing and empowering the act of giving and by spreading this notion across a community of friends and colleagues, society will be taking a significant step toward the transfer of wealth to those most in need.

GIVZ

Givz provides an API-powered platform that helps Shopify brands and other resellers by rewarding their customers with dollars to donate to a charity of their choice, driving conversion and increasing order value.

Headquarters and year founded: New York, 2017
Founder: Andrew Forman is a financial professional turned entrepreneur with a mission to elevate charitable giving through profitable enterprise. Formerly with Portico Capital, Bank of America, and Merrill Lynch,

Andrew has also been treasurer of a nonprofit promoting literacy in Ghana. Andrew graduated from Hamilton College and Harvard Business School.

Funds raised and VC investors: $3 million from Accomplice, Eniac Ventures.

Q&A WITH THE FOUNDER

Where did the idea for Givz originate?

The idea for Givz started formulating in my mind while I was treasurer of a nonprofit organization. People were commonly using Venmo to make contributions, and I was surprised that there was no Venmo equivalent for charitable giving. I then entered business school and decided that I wanted to go after this problem once I graduated. Based on some initial testing and feedback with a couple of brands, the business model evolved into a platform for allowing people to decide what charities to donate to as part of an e-commerce transaction. We did some A/B testing through Facebook and email and discovered that retailers that promoted charitable donations as part of their purchase funnel performed 18–20 percent better. This was our "a-ha" moment.

What's the key problem that Givz intends to solve?

The Givz platform offers online retailers and other types of businesses to increase their sales and order value while at the same time increasing charitable donations by allowing customers to decide what cause their purchase will help to support. We create social impact and reduce dependency on discounts for sellers.

How are you most differentiated as a service?

We provide Shopify businesses of all sizes to convert sales and increase order value at a measurably increased rate by promoting charitable giving as part of the purchase process. Moreover, we provide a choice of over 175,000 nonprofit organizations that empower the seller's customers to determine what causes to support. Our platform is seamless to integrate with minimal technical effort.

What are the company's key accomplishments to date?

We have hit over $1 million in total given to charities that people care about and will do another $200,000 this quarter. That represents over 7,500 charities supported. We have also demonstrated for resellers that Givz increases average order value by an astonishing 10–30 percent, which validates our proposition that charitable giving is not only good for society but is simply good business. We are now in active discussions about implementing Givz with several major brand-name retailers.

What lies ahead for Givz?

We are planning to soon expand outside of Shopify. We've launched a platform-agnostic API where any industry can take action to allow their clients and customers to allocate dollars to a charity of choice. We will also be working to connect charities and brands in a much more efficient and effective way. Thousands of charities are getting unsolicited dollars, but our platform will allow brands to feature and partner more tightly with charities of choice. We want to send over one billion dollars to charity in the next couple of years. This is the driving force for our team, wanting to make "giving" profitable.

RON'S TAKE

Promoting charitable giving hardly seems like a controversial idea. Individuals do it. Companies do it. We all have causes that we believe in. The innovation that Givz sheds light on is that charitable giving is also a profit-generating initiative. As an e-commerce company or really any type of business, the more customers are empowered to help direct part of their purchase to a cause that they choose, the more they will engage and purchase. Amazon Smile is one of the most notable examples of this, but the idea should apply across the board to nearly any business, large or small. The need is immense, and businesses will be well served by engaging more with their customers to direct capital and shine a spotlight on causes their customers care about. The Givz platform is there to enable companies to do this.

GOODWORLD

Goodworld provides a platform for social fundraising that works with non-profits, as well as companies and their employees, to make charitable donations simple and secure.

Headquarters and year founded: Washington, DC, 2015
Founder: Dale Nirvani Pfeifer, founder and CEO, is a leader in social impact and applying technology to help cultivate philanthropy and volunteerism. She has worked across research, communications, and leadership in the realms of politics, academia, and for-profit and nonprofit organizations. Dale holds bachelor's and master's degrees in psychology and management from Massey University in New Zealand.
Funds raised and VC investors: $4 million from 76 Forward, Astia, Camp One Ventures, Fenway Summer Ventures, Icehouse Ventures, MasterCard, Nyca Partners.

Q&A WITH THE FOUNDER

Where did the idea for Goodworld originate?

I have been involved in social causes since I came to the U.S. from New Zealand 15 years ago. I worked at a nonprofit in New York City and also conducted research at the Harvard Kennedy School alongside Professor David Gergen. In studying philanthropic giving and fundraising, I observed how friends were giving money with a very different mindset from how organizations were raising money. I felt that technology could be a bridge, and I wanted to create a company with a broad mandate to bring philanthropy to younger donors.

What's the key problem that Goodworld intends to solve?

Goodworld is about increasing philanthropic giving through engagement with nonprofits, companies, and employees. We do this by making giving a social experience that creates buzz and virality through social media and also by making donating a tool for employee engagement. We provide corporate social responsibility (CSR) and ESG software to companies as well as an engagement platform built for nonprofits.

How are you most differentiated as a service?

We have created a full system that companies can implement that allows employees to choose organizations that they wish to support alongside employer contributions. It is a turnkey platform with a menu of ten features that employers can offer, which includes tracking features, matching grants, and corporate skills-based volunteering. We've partnered with Salesforce to offer a seamless CRM that can be easily implemented by any organization.

What are the company's key accomplishments to date?

We have implemented our platform with eight companies so far, with more onboarding soon. We have 4,000 charities that manage social engagement through our cost-effective platform for nonprofits. We also have 1.7 million charities onboard that donors can select from. We are working with both large enterprises and SMEs across a wide range of industries.

What lies ahead for Goodworld?

We have big plans to grow our team and our partnerships that will help the cause of growing charitable giving. We will continue to offer more features, especially on the ESG side.

RON'S TAKE

This book covers many aspects of how startup companies are solving issues of wealth inequality that relate to money, health, education, housing, food security, and the like. However, it is also important to consider the actions that anyone with the means can help. The simplest and most tried and true way of doing this is simply by contributing a small amount of one's savings or income to the causes that they most believe in. Nothing revolutionary there.

However, innovative companies such as Goodworld, Cauze, and Givz are elevating the status of the giver and bringing a social dynamic that has proven to increase engagement and overall donation sizes. Goodworld's founder Dale Nirvani Pfeifer is an energetic voice whose company will empower nonprofits as they engage their supporters and businesses looking to put power in the hands of employees to decide where their contributions can best be put to use.

13

THE ROAD AHEAD

I hope that a decade from now, most venture capital dollars will be deployed into companies that are solving real problems that cut across the socioeconomic rungs of society. The overlooked majority, or the "base of the pyramid," are those who have been dealt less fortunate cards and where challenges are most acute, but almost most solvable. The biggest obstacle for getting there is educating potential investors that profitable investments can be made and the opportunities are sitting right before their eyes.

Since the rise of global capitalism in the post-World War II era, it has become an accepted mantra that there's little money to be made in low-income communities or emerging markets. In the United States, we've seen this most egregiously in the form of blatant redlining by banks, supermarkets, and other big consumer businesses of Black and low-income communities. Profits can be made more easily in the suburbs, the argument went, so why should we bother with inner cities and distant rural areas?

Impact investors who seek market returns have found they can align their values with the allocation of capital to address environmental and social issues. They can invest their money into businesses, funds, and nonprofits in education, healthcare, housing, microfinance, renewable energy, and sustainable agriculture. They do not consider their investments to be a form of charity—in fact, they often see their impact investments outperform their standard benchmarks.

To be sure, not all impact investors have the same financial goals. They can be divided into three groups: market rate, who expect impact investing to provide the same returns as any other approach; below market rate, who expect a lower return than conventional investing; and market rate, closer to capital preservation, where they expect performance no better than the safest conventional investment.

A survey done by the Global Impact Investing Network (GIIN) revealed that socially responsible investing tends to meet the expectations of each of the three types of investors. As the *2020 Annual Impact Investor Survey* stated, "An overwhelming majority of respondents reported meeting or exceeding both their impact expectations and their financial expectations... Performance relative to expectations, and especially reported financial performance, varied by investor subgroup. Just 8 percent of market-rate investors reported underperforming their financial performance expectations." [44] This suggests that 92 percent of market-rate investors thought their investments performed as expected—not a bad outcome!

Many impact investors measure their ROI as a "blended return." The concept was popularized by Jed Emerson to describe environmental, social, and financial value created by an organizations' activities because "value cannot be bifurcated and is inherently made up of more than one measurement of performance."[45]

It's also called the triple bottom line. The trio consists of the following:

Profit. No surprise here. No investor wants to lose money because, even if you're deeply dedicated to progressive causes, if you fail to make a profit, you'll soon be out of the game, and that doesn't do anyone any good.

People. We don't mean just the shareholders but also the stakeholders, including customers, employees, and members of the community. Simple ways companies can benefit their stakeholders include ensuring fair hiring practices, offering benefits such as paid maternity and paternity leave, encouraging volunteerism in the workplace, and forging successful strategic partnerships with nonprofit organizations that share a common purpose-driven goal.

The Planet. Even though businesses have historically contributed the most to climate change and pollution, they also hold the keys to creating positive change. This effort isn't the sole responsibility of the world's largest corporations—virtually all businesses have opportunities to make changes that reduce their carbon footprint. Adjustments like cutting down on energy consumption and using renewables, using ethically sourced materials, purchasing carbon credits, and streamlining shipping practices are measures most businesses can take.

GIIN's surveys show that nine out of ten investors who seek to have an impact have also achieved financial returns that meet or exceed their expectations. At the same time, an overwhelming 99 percent believe that the impact of their investment dollars met or exceeded expectations. For private equity investors, including venture capital, those surveyed who sought only impact investments reported gross annualized returns over an extended period dating back six decades of 17 percent, compared to a 16 percent gross annualized return for investors who pursued a mix of impact and non-impact investments.[46]

Mitch Kapor is a software industry pioneer, having co-founded Lotus Development Corporation and invented one of the first spreadsheets, Lotus 1-2-3. Over the past 12 years, he and his wife, Freada Kapor Klein, have operated Kapor Capital, one of the most active impact VC firms in the world. Kapor champions the notion that investing to maximize social impact and investing to maximize financial returns are not in conflict with one another. While focusing on investing in diverse founders and bringing to market technology solutions to some of the world's biggest equity gaps, they have also realized financial returns that have been in the top quartile of the VC industry for funds of their size.

The elephant in the room of social impact investing is and has always been the presumed tradeoff between societal and financial returns. To Mitch Kapor, this supposed conflict is nothing more than mythology, just as people once thought the world was flat or that certain racial groups were inferior. His firm has built a track record of investing in over 100 companies, including Altro, and Daivergent, profiled in this book, which were started by individuals who saw problems firsthand and found smart, new solutions to closing the gaps that led to them, and doing so with scalable technology.

As Kapor asserts, entrepreneurs tend to scratch their own itch, but if investors have not had similar life experiences or cannot relate to the problems personally, they often do not understand either the magnitude of the issue or what kind of solution is needed and how best to bring it to market. Many diverse founders, Kapor observes, are not born on second or third base and must make extra efforts to prove their worthiness to investors. A significant share of VC investors, however, come instead from more privileged backgrounds and are not necessarily drawn to the same life problems as the founders who are solving problems for the bottom of the pyramid.

Since the 2020 murder of George Floyd, Kapor has been approached by many fellow investors who have expressed a desire to invest more in diverse founders and business models that help to address equality gaps. This is gratifying to see, but results will come only through action. The entire venture ecosystem needs to focus more attention on bringing the representation of founders, investors, and new talent into the industry who have previously been overlooked. As Kapor states, Kapor Capital does not sacrifice discipline to invest in diverse teams and ideas. "We have a rigorous methodology that looks at markets, competition, founder grit, and coachability to determine where to invest. The good news is that there is no shortage of opportunities. We, as investors, just need to put ourselves out there and determine which of those founders and opportunities are likely to generate the greatest rewards, both financially and socially. We work closely with the founders that we invest in and take ownership in doing all that we can to support them in their journey."

Increasingly, investors are finding that the triple bottom line provides the best of all worlds—a good profit with a clear conscience. Serial entrepreneur-turned-investor Dr. Venkat Srinivasan believes that for-profit ventures are indeed the best avenue for creating innovation that supports social change. As managing director of Innospark Ventures in Boston, he has put money behind dozens of companies that are applying AI and other innovations for the betterment of humanity. His investments have had a global reach and include healthcare and education startups covered in this book, such as BrightUp, Creda Health, and EnglishHelper. Venkat looks at the intersection of social good and profit with a lens toward solvability by software and technology, a vast market size with an unmet need, an ability to dramatically lower cost, and the right person to lead, who is someone with the passion to be impactful.

Srinivasan states that the reality is that there is no reason why impact investments should have to sacrifice ROI. If an investor aims to solve a major problem, such as disease prevention, the goals of profit and impact are not in conflict. He points out that major problems generally have a massive market need, and it is in the entrepreneur's economic interests to maximize reach and not unit profit. He shares the view of Mitch Kapor that most entrepreneurs with a social mission are solving a problem that is based on some lived experience. For problems at the "bottom of the pyramid," however, many wealthy investors, including angels and VCs, have not had to face many of the challenges that exist there. Therefore, investors must recognize the opportunities and determine to address them through the investments they choose to make.

There is one more challenge to be met: the challenge of creating more diversity among investors themselves. It's no secret that venture capital has traditionally been the arena of white men investing in companies founded by other white men. As the *Stanford Social Innovation Review* noted in August 2021, "the venture capital industry is led by a highly uniform group of white, elite-educated men; [in fact,] 40 percent of venture capitalists in the U.S. are graduates of just two schools, Harvard and Stanford. Only 10 percent of VC partners in the U.S. are female, and not even 1 percent are Black."[47]

On the other side of the equation, women, Black, LGBTQ, and other minority entrepreneurs have found it difficult to get funding. Why is this? People like to invest in ventures that make them feel comfortable (a tendency academics call homophily), meaning that they fund ventures for and about people who look and act as they do.

The solution to this is twofold: The first is to broaden the horizons of white male investors and break down the cultural and societal barriers, including systemic racism, that play a role in reduced funding opportunities for minority entrepreneurs. The second solution is to look at it from the other side and eliminate systematic racism that stifles Black wealth building, thereby increasing the ranks of Black and minority people who themselves can become venture capital investors.

The good news is that higher-purpose investing is growing from the bottom up. By that, I mean many venture capital investors, from individual savers to large institutions, are looking to use their capital to help create a more sustainable world and are therefore directing an ever-increasing proportion of their portfolios towards sustainable strategies. They care about the world and have recognized that companies, which were once seen as money machines with no regard to their social and environmental cost, could be forces for good in the world while turning a healthy profit.

We're slowly seeing a gender shift in venture capital, with women stepping to the forefront as investors, corporate executives, and industry leaders. Women are also more likely to look at the big picture and seek to invest in companies that make a positive impact on the world. An RBC Wealth Management study found that "women are more than twice as likely as men to say it's extremely important that the companies they invest in incorporate ESG factors into their policies and procedures."[48]

One such leader in venture capital is Alda Leu Dennis, General Partner of San Francisco-based Initialized Capital Management, a venture firm with over $3 billion of AUM. Dennis constantly thinks about her investments with an impact lens, although she admits that the word "impact" comes with the baggage of the mythology that "impact" inversely correlates with "returns." She believes that founders will also work to solve big problems, but that capital flow into many ventures that are tackling societal issues are met with resistance simply because many investors are not motivated to act. Dennis feels that if venture fund limited partners (traditionally, pension funds, endowments, corporations, and family offices, among others) push VCs to focus on "double bottom line" investments, then they will be driven to act.

Much like Dennis, Dr. Joy Ippolito of the single-LP venture fund American Family Insurance Institute for Corporate and Social Impact seeks a personal connection and dual motivation for profit and purpose. Before becoming an impact investor, she spent nearly 20 years of her life as a licensed social worker, researcher, professor, and state policymaker in various systems, including education, juvenile justice, child welfare, and healthcare. "I had the humbling privilege of getting very proximate to individual lives and the stories that brought them to where they were. Each of these career experiences, coupled with my own lived experiences, provides a different lens and vantage point from which to understand the world and drives how I look at each possible venture deal. An investment that only has financial upside but minimal to no impact on closing an equity gap doesn't get very far in our pipeline. Neither does a startup that has massive social impact but lacks a business plan to create meaningful venture return. They need to be equal."

Because of her career experiences, Ippolito has a good handle on where innovation is sorely needed. "I also know where it's going to be challenging to implement a business model that can truly scale. It's a careful dance, especially in early-stage investing. While venture will always carry risk, I believe it is possible to eliminate some of that risk by not simply throwing money at everyone who exclaims, 'Here's a big problem, and here's a solution! Let's make some money!' Instead, we need to fund founders who say, 'I understand this problem and have built a thoughtful solution to help solve for it.' It may seem subtle, but in my experience, the intent and approaches are vastly different."

Investors and fund managers are getting help from technology, specifically AI, which can collect and analyze massive amounts of corporate data and provide better insights into how companies are being run from a higher-purpose perspective. For example, if an investor has a particular interest in climate change, AI can survey and identify emerging companies that are developing climate change solutions and helping the transition to a low-carbon economy.

AI can also help spot those companies engaged in "greenwashing"—enticing an aspiring green consumer or investor by pretending to be sustainable, socially responsible, or environmentally conscious while pursuing "business as usual." Investors are demanding more valuable insights into whether companies are truthful in their claimed ESG principles and want concrete answers about exactly how companies are improving inclusive hiring practices or reducing their carbon footprint, for example. In fact, in December 2022, joint oversight committees of the U.S. House of Representatives found that "despite public promises that fossil fuels [were] merely a 'bridge fuel' to cleaner sources of energy", the big oil companies had actually "doubled down on long-term reliance on fossil fuels with no intention of taking concrete actions to transition to clean energy."[49]

Evidence is mounting that socially responsible behavior is very good business—both on the VC and startup sides. A groundbreaking study by *Harvard Business Review* showed that increased diversity in VC decision-making teams—the people who provide the cash—leads to increased profitability both at the portfolio and overall fund level in venture capital firms. As my former professor Paul Gompers and research associate Silpa Kovvali reported, "The more similar the investment partners, the lower their investments' performance. For example, the success rate of acquisitions and IPOs was 11.5 percent lower, on average, for investments by partners with shared school backgrounds than for those by partners from different schools. The effect of shared ethnicity was even stronger, reducing an investment's comparative success rate by 26.4 percent to 32.2 percent."[50] Gender matters, too; VC firms that "increased their proportion of female partner hires by 10 percent saw, on average, a 1.5 percent spike in overall fund returns each year and had 9.7 percent more profitable exits."[51]

The difference wasn't so much in the startups that the VC teams chose to fund. Instead, the differences emerged when the VC team got involved in management, which many do. When the investors help shape strategy, recruitment, and other efforts critical to a young company's survival and growth, having a diverse set of viewpoints becomes a strategic advantage. To make it simple, when a male graduate from Harvard and a female grad from Hometown State College collaborate to reach a common goal, they make a powerful partnership.

When VC firms and individual investors become more diverse, they become more willing and interested in finding target companies that reflect their own makeup. This will become a virtuous cycle, leading to more higher-purpose investors reaching out to more higher-purpose companies and spreading economic opportunity to every corner of our great nation.

Purpose-driven venture investors have begun to proliferate in recent years. Many of these are led by emerging fund managers with a particular area of social interest. Examples include:

- Female founders (Female Founders Fund, Graham & Walker, Pink Salt Ventures, Springbank Collective)
- Diverse founders (1863 Ventures, Collide Capital, Harlem Capital, Impact America Fund, One Way Ventures, VamosVentures, Softbank Opportunity Fund)
- Education (Owl Ventures, Reach Capital, Rethink Capital Partners)
- Public health (Adjuvant Capital, MBX Capital)
- Climate tech (Astanor Ventures, Breakthrough Energy Ventures, Clean Energy Ventures, regenr8, The Westly Group)
- Disabilities (Enable Ventures)
- Broad ESG mandate, including social and economic mobility (DBL Partners, Emerson Collective, Gratitude Railroad, Kapor Capital, Omidyar Network, Social Impact Capital)

What unifies all these firms is their aligned strategies of maximizing impact without sacrificing returns. Today, over 100 venture capital firms make social impact a prominent feature of their mandate. This demonstrates that their

LPs are stepping up, believing their money can do good for the world while generating a meaningful financial return.

This volume is intended as a clarion call to fellow venture investors. Use your investable capital for good. Deploy where you can have a lasting impact and a legacy to be proud of for your children and grandchildren. One does not need to sacrifice financial returns to support and empower overlooked entrepreneurs to solve problems built for those who do not come from wealth and privilege. If an investor is considering whether it makes sense to invest with an impact lens, one could ask a simple question: "If given the choice to invest in a company that manufactures and sells tobacco or a company that is developing a cure for cancer, which would I choose?"

There are entrepreneurs all around the world who are actively developing solutions that are scalable, innovative, and globally relevant. They solve problems that are faced by humanity's vast lower to middle class, covering Maslow's most basic needs, from health to housing, food security, financial literacy, job skills, basic education, and more. They address the challenges of women, minorities, people of color, immigrants, and those with disabilities. By and large, the founders of these companies have a personal connection to the challenge they are solving.

For investors, the plan of action starts with identifying the scope of where and how to invest. Whether investing as an angel, a VC, a lender, or otherwise, one should consider the following:

1) *What causes do I most care about?* Is it education, healthcare, food and water, housing, job security, professional development, or financial independence? Should I focus on women, people of color, individuals with disabilities, or a combination thereof? Do I want to focus on a particular geographic region of the country or of the world?

2) *At what stage can I be most helpful with capital and providing advice?* Do I like working with very early-stage entrepreneurs to help them build an idea, find product-market fit, identify a team, and put building blocks in place? Or do I prefer to invest with founders who have already identified a proven idea but are ready to take it to a broader scale and have a lasting impact?

3) *What level of risk shall I take to seek double bottom line rewards?* As with any type of alternative asset, particularly private company venture

investing, there is risk, and it requires patience. Investments are typically illiquid for 5–10 years or more, and there is rarely a straight path from startup to success. Many ventures will ultimately fail due to any number of reasons. Most investors will therefore spread their capital across dozens or even hundreds of investments. Diversification is not just a good idea from a portfolio management perspective. It is good from an impact standpoint to empower even more entrepreneurs to solve more problems from different angles and with varying approaches.

There is no lack of such entrepreneurs willing to take on these problems and devise groundbreaking solutions. What we need more of are dollars to support them, which come from venture capitalists, angel investors, family offices, and other wealthy individuals. Often, these investors, on a personal level, have not had to face the problems they are being asked to solve. However, that doesn't mean that they can't clearly see the opportunities. As has been shared, investors are already putting their money to work on these issues. To have a greater lasting impact, those dollars need to flow even faster. The good news is there is no conflict between doing good and doing well.

It's the future of VC investing—and it's here today.

THANK YOU

T hank you for reading this book. I would like to acknowledge all the entrepreneurs and fellow investors who I had the great privilege of interview-
ing for this book. They have been an inspiration and what kept me going
and focused as I published my blogs and prepared this book.

To continue this journey, please follow my Higher Purpose Venture
Capital Blog at ronlevin.substack.com.

ENDNOTES

1   Mitchell, Travis. "Trends in Income and Wealth Inequality." Pew Research Center's Social & Demographic Trends Project. Pew Research Center, August 17, 2020. https://www.pewresearch.org/social-trends/2020/01/09/trends-in-income-and-wealth-inequality/.

2   Alexander, Michelle. *The New Jim Crow: Mass Incarceration in the Age of Colorblindness.* New York: The New Press, 2011.

3   McFarland, Susan. "U.N. report: With 40M in poverty, U.S. most unequal developed nation." UPI. June 22, 2018. https://www.upi.com/Top_News/US/2018/06/22/UN-report-With-40M-in-poverty-US-most-unequal-developed-nation/8671529664548/?spt=su.

4   Ostland, Andrew. "What the coming $68 trillion Great Wealth Transfer means for financial advisors." CNBC. October 21, 2019. https://www.cnbc.com/2019/10/21/what-the-68-trillion-great-wealth-transfer-means-for-advisors.html#:~:text=Cerulli%20Associates%20estimates%20that%20as,after%20inheriting%20their%20parents'%20wealth.#:~:text=Cerulli%20Associates%20estimates%20that%20as,after%20inheriting%20their%20parents'%20wealth.###############

5   PwC. "ESG-focused institutional investment seen soaring 84% to US$33.9 trillion in 2026, making up 21.5% of assets under management: PwC report." PwC. October 10, 2022. https://www.pwc.com/gx/en/news-room/press-releases/2022/awm-revolution-2022-report.html

6   Bloomberg Professional Services. "The future of ESG: A conversation with GPIF Chief Investment Officer Hiro Mizuno." Bloomberg, May 19, 2019. https://www.bloomberg.com/professional/blog/future-esg-conversation-gpif-chief-investment-officer-hiro-mizuno/

7   UBS. "ESG and Sustainability." n.d. https://www.ubs.com/global/en/investment-bank/what-we-offer/esg.html

8   TPG. "TPG's Annual ESG Review: Environmental, Social and Governance Performance." TPG. March 31, 2022. https://cms.tpg.com/wp-content/uploads/2022/08/TPG-ESG-Report-2022_FINAL.pdf

9   RSM US LLP. "Why ESG matters to family offices." RSM. January 25, 2022. https://realeconomy.rsmus.com/why-esg-matters-to-family-offices/

10 Bridges Fund. "Our Story." Bridges Fund Management. n.d. https://www.bridgesfundmanagement.com/us/our-story/

11 So, Rachel. "5 Facts about the World's Unbanked Population." The Borgen Project. June 3, 2022. https://borgenproject.org/unbanked-population/

[12] BPC. "Digital banking in Africa report by BPC highlights challenges and opportunities in Sub-Saharan region where over 50% are unbanked." BPC, March 17, 2022. https://www.bpcbt.com/blog/digital-bank-in-africa-report-by-bpc#:~:text=While%20 there%20have%20been%20positive,account%2C%20including%20mobile%20 money%20accounts.

[13] Beck, Thorsten, Samuel Munzele Maimbo, Issa Faye, and Thouraya Triki. "Financing Africa: Through the Crisis and Beyond." The International Bank for Reconstruction and Development, The World Bank. 2011.https://www.worldbank.org/en/programs/africa-regional-studies/publication/financing-africa-through-the-crisis-and-beyond

[14] "9th Annual Parents, Kids & Money Survey." T. Rowe Price. 2017. https://www.moneyconfidentkids.com/us/en/news-and-research/research/2017-parents--kids---money-survey-results.html

[15] "PISA 2015 Results (Volume IV): Students' Financial Literacy." PISA, OECD. May 24, 2017. https://www.oecd.org/education/pisa-2015-results-volume-iv-9789264270282-en.htm

[16] Simmons, Christian. "Financial Literacy in the Black Community." Annuity.org. Last modified March 2, 2023. https://www.annuity.org/financial-literacy/black-community/

[17] "Education pays." U.S. Bureau of Labor Statistics. Last modified September 8, 2022. https://www.bls.gov/emp/tables/unemployment-earnings-education.htm

[18] "Chronic Absenteeism in the Nation's Scools." U.S. Department of Education. Last modified on October 27, 2016. https://www2.ed.gov/datastory/chronicabsenteeism.html#:~:text=Understanding%20when%20students%20are%20most,of%20 students%20in%20middle%20school.

[19] "Career and Technical Education Programs Face Challenges In Preparing the Future Workforce." U.S. Government Accountability Office. April 7, 2022. https://www.gao.gov/blog/career-and-technical-education-programs-face-challenges-preparing-future-workforce

[20] Michel, Sonya. "The History of Child Care in the U.S." Social Welfare History Project. 2011. https://socialwelfare.library.vcu.edu/programs/child-care-the-american-history/

[21] Henderson, Tim. "Investors Bought a Quarter of Homes Sold Last Year, Driving Up Rents." Pew Charitable Trusts. July 22, 2022. https://www.pewtrusts.org/en/research-and-analysis/blogs/stateline/2022/07/22/investors-bought-a-quarter-of-homes-sold-last-year-driving-up-rents.

[22] "Brown: Our Housing Market Should Serve Renters and Communities—Not Private Equity's Bottom Lines." United States Senate Committee on Banking, Housing, and Urban Affairs. February 10, 2022. https://www.banking.senate.gov/newsroom/majority/brown-our-housing-market-should-serve-renters-and-communities_not-private-equitys-bottom-lines

[23] Schaul, Kevin and Jonathan O'Connell. "Investors bought a record share of homes in 2021. See where." *The Washington Post*. February 16, 2022. https://www.washingtonpost.com/business/interactive/2022/housing-market-investors/

[24] Connley, Courtney. "Why the homeownership gap between White and Black Americans is larger today than it was over 50 years ago." CNBC. August 21, 2020. https://www.cnbc.com/2020/08/21/why-the-homeownership-gap-between-white-and-black-americans-is-larger-today-than-it-was-over-50-years-ago.html

[25] Axel-Lute, Miriam. "What is NIMBYism and How Do Afordable Housing Developers Respond to It?" Shelterforce. November 17, 2021. https://shelterforce.

org/2021/11/17/what-is-nimbyism-and-how-do-affordable-housing-developers-respond-to-it/#:~:text=NIMBY%20stands%20for%20%E2%80%9CNot%20in,denser%20or%20more%20affordable%20housing.

26 Quick, Susie. "A Town Called Malnourished." *Newsweek*. April 3, 2014. https://www.newsweek.com/town-called-malnourished-248087

27 Zhang, Mengyao and Ghosh Debarchana. "Spatial Supermarket Redlining and Neighborhood Vulnerability: A Case Study of Hartford, Connecticut." National Library of Medicine. March 26, 2015. https://www.ncbi.nlm.nih.gov/pmc/articles/PMC4810442/#:~:text=%E2%80%9CSupermarket%20redlining%E2%80%9D%20is%20a%20term,to%20suburbs%20(Eisenhauer%202001).

28 "Food Waste and Food Rescue." Feeding America. n.d. https://www.feedingamerica.org/our-work/reduce-food-waste#:~:text=How%20much%20food%20waste%20is,food%20in%20America%20is%20wasted.

29 "Diarrhoeal disease." World Health Organization. May 2, 2017. Diarrhoeal disease (who.int).

30 "The Decline of Primary Care: The Silent Crisis Undermining U.S. Health Care." PNHP. August 9, 2011. https://pnhp.org/2011/08/09/the-decline-of-primary-care-the-silent-crisis-undermining-u-s-health-care/

31 "Rebecca Love, Experienced Nurse Innovator and Entrepreneur, Joins the Nurse-1-1 Board of Directors." Nurse-1-1. April 28, 2022. https://nurse-1-1.com/health/rebecca-love-experienced-nurse-innovator-and-entrepreneur-joins-the-nurse-1-1-board-of-directors/.

32 "Our Story." Zócalo Health. n.d. https://www.zocalo.health/about.

33 Davies, Dave. "How the 1965 Immigration Act Made America A Nation of Immigrants." NPR. January 16, 2019. https://www.npr.org/2019/01/16/685819397/how-the-1965-immigration-act-made-america-a-nation-of-immigrants.

34 "Press Release: New Study Reveals Immigrants Are Behind More Than Three-Quarters of Patents From Top Ten Patent-Producing American Universities." Partnership for a New American Economy. June 26, 2012. https://www.newamericaneconomy.org/news/press-release-new-study-reveals-immigrants-behind-three-quarters-patents-top-ten-patent-producing-american-universities/.

35 "NFAP Policy Brief: Immigrants and Nobel Prizes: 1901–2021." National Foundation for American Policy. October 2021. https://nfap.com/wp-content/uploads/2021/10/Immigrants-and-Nobel-Prizes-1901-to-2021.NFAP-Policy-Brief.October-2021.pdf.

36 Wisenberg Brin, Dinah. "Immigrants Form 25% of New U.S. Businesses, Driving Entrepreneurship in 'Gateway' States." *Forbes*. July 31, 2018. https://www.forbes.com/sites/dinahwisenberg/2018/07/31/immigrant-entrepreneurs-form-25-of-new-u-s-business-researchers/?sh=107d1247713b

37 Anderson, Stuart. "Immigrant Entrepreneurs And U.S. Billion-Dollar Companies." National Foundation for American Policy. July 2022. https://nfap.com/wp-content/uploads/2022/07/2022-BILLION-DOLLAR-STARTUPS.NFAP-Policy-Brief.2022.pdf

38 Salazar Genovez, Ruben. "The human impact of cross-border remittances." Visa. December 17, 2021. https://usa.visa.com/visa-everywhere/blog/bdp/2021/12/16/the-human-impact-1639694873289.html.

39 Ong, Rebecca. "Remittances Grow 5% in 2022, Despite Global Headwinds." The World Bank. November 30, 2022. https://www.worldbank.org/en/news/press-release/2022/11/30/remittances-grow-5-percent-2022

40 Burgstahler, Sheryl. "The Role of Technology in Preparing Youth with Disabilities for Postsecondary Education and Employment." *Journal of Special Education Technology*, 18, no. 4 (Fall 2003). https://www.researchgate.net/profile/Sheryl-Burgstahler/publication/230853091_The_Role_of_Technology_in_Preparing_Youth_with_Disabilities_for_Postsecondary_Education_and_Employment/links/55943e2f08ae21086d1ecd2f/The-Role-of-Technology-in-Preparing-Youth-with-Disabilities-for-Postsecondary-Education-and-Employment.pdf#page=8

41 Rouse, William B. and Dennis K. McBride. "A Systems Approach to Assistive Technology for Disabled and Older Adults." *The Bridge*, 49, no. 1 (March 2019). National Academy of Engineering. https://www.nae.edu/19579/19582/21020/205212/205332/A-Systems-Approach-to-Assistive-Technologies-for-Disabled-and-Older-Adults.

42 "What is AT?" Assisstive Technology Industry Association. n.d. https://www.atia.org/home/at-resources/what-is-at/

43 Schulte, Taylor. "Charitable Giving Statistics for 2023." Define Financial. February 10, 2023. https://www.definefinancial.com/blog/charitable-giving-statistics/

44 Hand, Dean, Hannah Dithrich, Sophia Sunderji, and Noshin Nova. "2020 Annual Impact Investor Survey." Global Impact Investing Network. June 11, 2020. 2020 Annual Impact Investor Survey | The GIIN.

45 Chowdhury, Anshula. "Calculating the Return of Your Impact Investment." Sametrica. March 7, 2022. https://sametrica.com/blog/calculating-return-impact-investing/.

46 Hand, Dean, Sophia Sunderji, Noshin Nova, and Indrani De. "Impact Investing Decision-making: Insights on Financial Performance." Global Impact Investing Network. January 14, 2021. Impact Investing Decision-making: Insights on Financial Performance | The GIIN

47 Lenhard, Johannes and Susan Winterberg. "How Venture Capital Can Join the USG Revolution." Stanford Social Innovation Review. August 26, 2021. https://ssir.org/articles/entry/how_venture_capital_can_join_the_esg_revolution#

48 "Women are leading the charge for Environmental, Social and Governance (ESG) investing in the U.S. amid growing demand for responsible investing solutions." RBC Wealth Management. April 6, 2021. https://www.rbcwealthmanagement.com/en-us/newsroom/2021-04-06/women-are-leading-the-charge-for-environmental-social-and-governance-esg-investing-in-the-us-amid-growing-demand-for-responsible-investing-solutions

49 "Oversight Committee Releases New Documents Showing Big Oil's Greenwashing Campaign and Failure to Reduce Emissions." House Committee on Oversight and Accountability. December 9, 2022. https://oversightdemocrats.house.gov/news/press-releases/oversight-committee-releases-new-documents-showing-big-oil-s-greenwashing.

50 Gompers, Paul and Silpa Kovvali. "The Other Diversity Dividend." *Harvard Business Review*, July–August 2018.https://hbr.org/2018/07/the-other-diversity-dividend.

51 Ibid.

Printed in the USA
CPSIA information can be obtained
at www.ICGtesting.com
CBHW010152121123
1746CB00007B/2

9 781960 142382